CW00793692

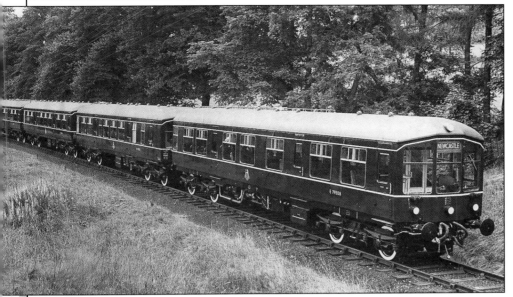

In pristine ex-works condition, one of the five 'Derby Lightweight' four-car units is posed for the official BR camera. Motor composite driving cars No E79508 and No E79509 flank the two trailers, third-class brake No E79325 and third-class No E79400. The driving cars each had 20 first class and 36 third class seats, while the trailer third-class brake and the third-class trailer vehicles, respectively, accommodated 45 and 61 third class ticket holders. *Ian Allan Library*

Now with 'speed whiskers', two 'Derby Lightweight' twin DMUs wind away from Harwich Parkeston Quay station on 7 April 1958, forming the 16.48 service from Harwich Town to Manningtree. Driving trailer composite No E79261 leads motor brakes No E79045 and E79031, with another trailer composite No E79623 bringing up the rear. Both trailers contain 16 first class and 53 second class seats, the two motor brakes having 56 second class seats only. *John N. Faulkner*

Passing on the main line at Bentley on 18 July 1958, one 'Derby Lightweight' twin, forming a Wroxham local service, passes another which is attached to a two-car Metro-Cammell unit, and heads south as a return special working from Norwich to Romford; DMBS

No E79037 faces the camera. Both the early Metro-Cammell DMUs and the second batch of 'Derby Lightweights' had compatible 'yellow diamond' coupling arrangements.
G. R. Mortimer

Forming the 17.05 train to Penrith, a Derby twin departs from Carlisle on 16 May 1960, formed of DMBS No M79016 and DTC No M79612. *John N. Faulkner*

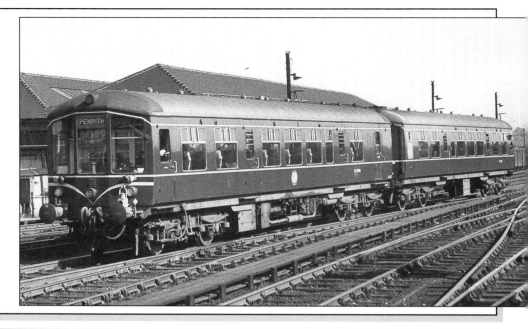

Forming the 11.50 service from Cambridge to Peterborough North, a Derby twin leaves Peterborough East station on 6 June 1960, with motor brake second No E79024 leading. *Michael Mensing*

A four-car 'Derby Lightweight' unit has strayed from its more usual Tyneside haunts, and prepares to depart from York on 30 November 1962, forming a service to Leeds. The leading driving motor No E79152 has seating for 64 second class ticket holders.
Michael Mensing

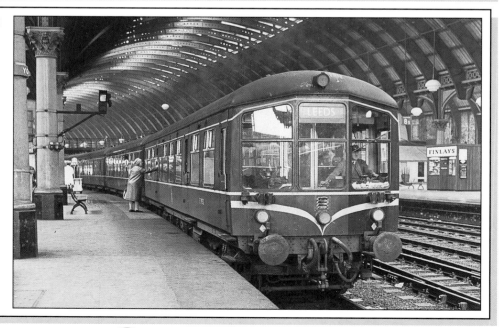

Formed of driving trailer composite No M79605 and motor brake second No M79015, the 11.55 Glasgow Central-Carlisle stopping train, via the Glasgow & South Western route, pauses for custom at Kilmarnock on 18 August 1966. The DTC is one containing only nine first class seats but with 53 available for second class ticket holders. The unit is still in lined-green livery, but a half-yellow warning panel has replaced the 'speed whiskers'.
A. Wyn Hobson

One of the motor brake driving cars with second class seating reduced in number from 61 to 56, No E79029 arrives at Sudbury on 26 June 1965 as the 11.07 service from Cambridge. The driving trailer, No E79258 attached, houses another 53 seats for second class, and has 16 available for any first class travellers. The route from Cambridge to Marks Tey and Colchester via Haverhill and Sudbury closed in 1967, returning Sudbury to its original status of a branch terminus.
John N. Faulkner

With half-melted snow on the roof, a 'Derby Lightweight' twin waits to leave Carlisle for Whitehaven on a bleak 23 January 1968. The yellow diamond coupling code on each lower corner of the unit's front end is particularly noticeable, and so is the mis-spelt destination blind! *John Glover*

Bound for Penrith, and pictured some two miles east of Keswick, driving trailer composite No M79648 heads a Derby twin in August 1965, with the superb scenery of the Lake District providing a backcloth to the scene. This line closed in March 1972. *W. J. V. Anderson*

A 'Derby Lightweight'/Metro-Cammell hybrid two-car DMU forms a Norwich to Cambridge train near Brandon on 16 May 1967. The Derby-built driving trailer has been painted into BR 'corporate blue', but has retained a 'half-yellow' warning panel, and has also lost its roof light. *C. F. Burton*

On 28 June 1968, a 'Derby Lightweight' twin forming the 18.13 Carlisle-Hawick local train slows for the Newcastleton stop. This was the last summer for Waverley route trains before closure of the line in January 1969. *Michael Mensing*

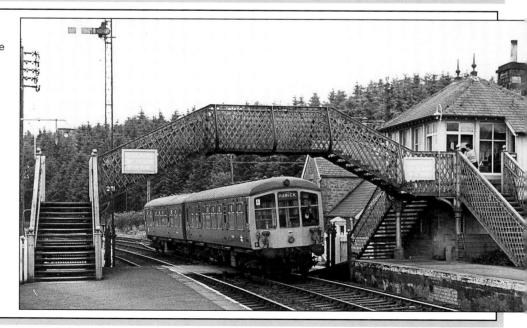

Passing Briery, east of Keswick, on 18 June 1968, driving trailer composite No M79645 heads the 12.25 train from Keswick to Penrith. To show first class passengers where their nine seats are situated, a painted line has been placed just below roof level.
Michael Mensing

Just one two-car 'Derby Lightweight' train still survives. Withdrawn from normal service in 1968, DMBS No M79018 and DMC No M79612 were converted for Departmental use as an Ultrasonic Test Train, and the cars renumbered DB970007 and 970008, respectively. The unit operated throughout the BR network, and provided Civil Engineers Department technicians with readouts of the track conditions over which they were passing. In this view of 4 March 1980, the unit is travelling through Twyford, with an eventual circuitous destination of Watford.
Colin J. Marsden

Stabled inside Stratford Depot on 7 July 1987, the unit is now painted into distinctive 'Derby Research' colours of red and blue. Withdrawn for a second time, the Derby twin has been purchased by the Derby Lightweight Preservation Group and is currently at the Midland Railway Centre, Derbyshire.

Metro-Cammell two-car 'Lightweight'

Built by:	Metropolitan-Cammell Carriage & Wagon Company
Introduced:	December 1955
Coupling Code:	Yellow Diamond ◆
Engines in each Driving Motor:	Two BUT (AEC) six-cylinder horizontal type 150hp
Transmission:	Mechanical, Standard
Body:	57ft 0in x 9ft 3in
Weight:	DMBT 26 tons 10cwt
	DTTL 25 tons
	DTCL 25 tons
Operating numbers:	DMBT 79047 to 79082
	DTTL 79263 to 79291
	DTCL 79626 to 79632

The 36 original Metro-Cammell two-car units were the first railcars to be ordered from an outside contractor. They had a specification similar to the second batch of 'Derby Lightweights', but their external appearance was totally different, setting the style which was to become unmistakably 'Metro-Cammell'. The majority of the sets were allocated to East Anglia, but seven were passed to the London Midland Region for use originally on the Bury-Bacup route. Although having a tendency not to ride too smoothly at speed, they gave good service until many of the lines on which they operated were closed. Having 'yellow diamond' coupling, they were compatible only with the 'Derby Lightweights' and Cravens LMR parcels cars of the same coupling code. This factor prevented their use elsewhere, and as a result, all the trains were withdrawn by June 1969. None have survived into preservation.

In original lined-green livery with 'lion and wheel' crests, the first Metro-Cammell units were constructed with four front-end marker lights, waist-height jumper cables, and were provided with a cowling beneath the bufferbeams which contained the air horn. With motor brake driving car No M79076 facing the camera, a newly-built unit is used for publicity purposes in December 1955, with 'Metro-Cammell' branding showing in the route indicator panel. *GEC Alsthom*

First series Metro-Cammell units under construction inside the company works at Washwood Heath in 1955. *GEC Alsthom*

Three-plus-two third (later second) class seating as contained in the Metro-Cammell 'Lightweight' units. *GEC Alsthom*

Two-plus-two seating in the first type of Metro-Cammell driving trailer composite. *GEC Alsthom*

Two Metro-Cammell 'Lightweight' twins leave Saxmundham on 26 April 1958, forming the 12.36 train from Aldeburgh to Ipswich. Driving trailer second No E79275 faces the camera, and is attached to motor brake driving cars No E79053 and No E79074 and fellow DTSL No E79269. To the right of the coupling can be seen the air horn protruding from the cowling. Passenger services to Aldeburgh ceased in September 1966. *John N. Faulkner*

On 7 April 1958, a first series Metro-Cammell twin stands in Brightlingsea branch terminus, forming the 13.20 train to St Botolphs. Motor brake driving car No E79058 leads driving trailer second No E79289. The Brightlingsea branch closed in June 1964. *John N. Faulkner*

A special working in conjunction with the King's Lynn Traders' Fair on 1 May 1958, leaves King's Lynn for Dereham. Motor brake driving car No E79061 is on the rear of the two-car unit. *Colin J. Marsden collection*

Forming an excursion from Southend-on-Sea to Portsmouth Harbour, Metro-Cammell and Derby 'Lightweight' two-car units are coupled together passing Surbiton on 8 June 1958. Metro-Cammell DMBS No E79068 leads DTSL No E79284, with the Derby unit formed of DMBS/DTCL Nos E79039/79255.
John N. Faulkner

Having arrived at Thetford with the branch train from Swaffham on a frosty 3 January 1959, a Metro-Cammell 'Lightweight' heads for the station crossover in order to change platforms for the return service. Sporting 'speed whiskers', DTSL No E79278 faces the camera. *Rodney Lissenden*

Only the seven Metro-Cammell 'Lightweights' originally allocated to the LMR for Bury-Bacup services were considered as requiring first class accommodation, and it is for this reason that just seven driving trailer composite vehicles were included in the fleet. These contained 12 first and 53 second class seats, compared with 71 second class only seats in the other 29 driving trailers sent to East Anglia. With 'Bacup' showing in the destination panel, one such car heads one of the LMR units at Bury in July 1956. Services to Bacup finished in December 1966.
C. R. Lewis Coles

With 'Wells' showing in the destination blind, a Metro-Cammell 'Lightweight' twin, with motor brake No E79054 providing power from the rear, makes the prescribed stop at Fakenham East in September 1962, forming a Wells-next-the-Sea to Dereham service. Trains on this line ceased to run in October 1964. *Stanley Creer*

With a half-yellow front warning panel replacing the 'speed whiskers', the 17.00 Manchester Piccadilly to Hayfield train near Strines on 19 June 1965, is formed of a Metro-Cammell 'Lightweight' twin, with motor brake No M79081 leading. The seven Midland Region motor brake seconds of this type were constructed with 53 seats, whereas their 29-strong Eastern Region counterpart had a slightly higher density with provision for 57. The branch from New Mills Central to Hayfield closed in January 1970. *Michael Mensing*

Forming a stopping train from Lowestoft to Norwich, a first series Metro-Cammell twin heads past the gated crossing controlled by Oulton Broad North Station signalbox, *circa* 1964. Unlike the previous illustration, the waist-height jumper control sockets just below the cab windows do not have cables fitted. *Stanley Creer*

BR Swindon three- and six-car 'Inter-City'

Built by:	BR Swindon Works
Introduced:	September 1956
Coupling Code:	White Circle ●
Engines in each Driving Motor:	Two BUT (AEC) six-cylinder horizontal type 150hp
Transmission:	Mechanical, Standard
Body:	64ft 6in x 9ft 3in
Weight:	DMBSL 38 tons
	DMSL 39 tons 3cwt
	TFBK 34 tons
	TFK 33 tons 9cwt
Operating numbers:	DMBSL 79083 to 79111
	DMSL 79155 to 79168
	TFBK 79440 to 79447
	TFK 79470 to 79482

Prior to its Modernisation Plan being announced, the British Transport Commission acted upon a 1952 committee report that recommended trials with express diesel railcars on the main line between Edinburgh and Glasgow, and asked Swindon Works to design and construct 21 three-car units for the service. These 'InterCity' DMUs were the first on BR to be built on 64½ft underframes, and were of steel construction, weighing considerably more than any of the 'Lightweight' units that had gone before. To allow for through gangway connections when units were coupled together, the DMBS cars were of two distinct types, the 'leading' vehicles having a full-width driving cab without a gangway connection, and the 'intermediate' power cars having a cab offset to one side to allow for a through gangway, a feature which also applied to the 14 DMSL vehicles. Interior layout for second class was in open style, side corridor compartments being provided for first class, which was situated in a non-powered trailer, and in some cases incorporated a buffet area. In traffic, the trains performed quite well on a 1hr timing with one intermediate stop between the two Scottish cities, although their riding qualities never matched the smooth running Gresley-bogied locomotive-hauled coaches they displaced. Further sets to the same basic design were ordered under the Modernisation Plan, and together with a number of the pioneer InterCity order, became Class 126. Displaced from the Edinburgh-Glasgow route by later railcars and locomotive-powered 'push-pull' services in 1970, most units were withdrawn in October 1972, although five power cars were sold out of service to a mining railway in Liberia, and a kitchen car was used for a time as a camping coach on the North Yorkshire Moors Railway. Power car No 79098 became a mess coach in Departmental Stock but has since been withdrawn, and the sole survivor is trailer first buffet car No 79443 on the Bo'ness & Kinneil Railway.

Having just emerged from Swindon Works, 'intermediate' DMBS No Sc79095 is posed for the official camera. Turned out in green livery with cream lining and a little 'speed whisker', there is no provision for either marker lights or a destination blind.
Ian Allan Library

Forming an excursion from Birmingham Snow Hill on 12 July 1958, two three-car Swindon 'Inter-City' sets arrive at Paddington and pass 'Castle' class 4-6-0 No 5039 *Rhuddlan Castle*, which is backing on to stock for the 'Pembroke Coast Express'. A 'leading' DMBS No W79092 heads TFK No W79473 and 'intermediate' DMBS No 79083, the second unit being formed in a similar fashion with vehicles Nos W79086/79441/79089. A total of 12 power cars and six kitchen cars were initially allocated to Western Region, but all were transferred to Scotland by 1962. In the absence of marker lights or a destination blind, a large stencilled letter 'A' for express passenger or 'B' for a semi-fast working was provided with back illumination. Oil lamps had to be carried for tail lights.
John N. Faulkner

Because of the gangway connection, the headcode panel on the 'intermediate' powercars had to be repeated on each side of the front end below the windows. Forming the 08.10 Birmingham Snow Hill-Carmarthen train, an original BR Swindon 'InterCity' six-car unit hares through Widney Manor station on 8 July 1959. *Michael Mensing*

The interior design of a Swindon buffet car looks something akin to a decorated wartime bomb shelter! The posed BR photograph was taken on 25 April 1957. *Ian Allan Library*

Trailer first buffet corridor (TFBK) No W79441 is the centre vehicle between Swindon powercars Nos 79083/79155. Branded 'Buffet', the vehicle also displays a coachboard for 'Birmingham Gloucester Cardiff Swansea & Carmarthen'. *P. J. Sharpe*

Considering they were the first 'Inter-City' units of the BR railcar programme, the Swindon front-end design for them was particularly bland, and evoked a rather curious sense of unnecessary postwar utility. Each individual unit car having been constructed to produce its own air supply, the trains had no through air pipe. In consequence, if the engine of a 'leading' car was out of commission for any reason, the horns which were placed beneath the buffer beam would not sound, and the unit would be treated as having failed, a fault that was later rectified. A six-car Birmingham-Paddington express approaches Ruislip on 24 August 1957, headed by DMBS No W79092. *C. R. Lewis Coles*

With a 'B' stencil on both sides of the corridor connection, 'intermediate' DMBS No W79089 leads an original three-car BR Swindon 'Inter-City' unit approaching Hatton on 18 June 1959. The train is the 20.00 service from Leamington Spa General to Birmingham Moor Street. *Michael Mensing*

Making the mandatory stop at Acocks Green & South Yardley station on 11 April 1959, 'intermediate' powercar No W79090 faces the camera with a three-car train forming the 13.20 from Birmingham Moor Street to Leamington Spa General. Both types of DMBSL had 52 second class seats, with the DMSL vehicles having 64. The first class seated 42, with the kitchen cars having 30 seats, 18 outside and 12 inside the buffet area. *Michael Mensing*

Now in blue and grey livery, a six-car Swindon 'InterCity' DMU passes Bo'ness Junction, between Linlithgow and Polmont, on 18 February 1971, forming the 14.00 service from Edinburgh to Glasgow Queen Street. The headcode box carries a solitary '1' in place of the original letter 'A' or 'B'. *G. A. Watt*

Two of the five Swindon-built 'Inter-City' Vehicles sold to Lamco Mining, Liberia, are posed there in Green Hill Quarry on 24 November 1982, No 79094 facing the camera. With Driver Pete Fisher in the cab, the cars have been given orange and white livery, 'cow catchers', and two front headlights. The allocated BR numbers were retained. *Mick Boyd.*

BUT three-car four-wheel 'Railbus'

Built by:	British United Traction Company
Introduced:	May 1952
Coupling Code:	None
Engines in each Driving Motor:	One BUT (AEC) six-cylinder horizontal type 125hp
Transmission:	Mechanical
Body:	37ft 6in x 9ft 0in
Weight:	DMT 15 tons
	DMBT 15 tons
	TT 10 tons 10cwt:
Operating numbers:	DMT 79740/45/48
	DMBT 79742/43/44/50
	TT 79741/46/47/49

A cross between a diesel multiple unit and a railbus, the first privately-sponsored three-car 'ACV Demonstration Train' was described by BR as combining the best features of both rail and road vehicles, and was the first four-wheel railcar to appear in the UK since the turn of the century. The bodywork was manufactured by Park Royal Vehicles Ltd, and the train was assembled by BUT, using their own mass-produced AEC engines of the type which powered London's 'Green Line' buses and many differing vehicles all over the world. Announced as the 'New British Lightweight Train', but quickly acquiring the sobriquet 'flying bricks', the first unit was put to work on the Chiltern Lines from Marylebone, followed by spells on other parts of the system including the Watford-St Albans Abbey line, the Harrow-Belmont branch and the Allhallows branch in Kent. As with ensuing two-axle passenger car

stock, the train was rough riding and uncomfortable, and had difficulty in operating track circuits, but was eventually sold for service on the London Midland Region which operated three sets of them from 1955. Withdrawn in February 1959, all the vehicles were eventually cut up at Derby Carriage Works in November 1963.

> Painted in two-tone grey livery with red lining, 'ACV Demonstration Railcars' Nos 1, 2 and 3 wait to depart from Watford Junction on 9 August 1952, forming the 17.48 service for St Albans Abbey. Purchased by the LMR in November 1953, the cars were renumbered out of sequence as M79742, M79740 and M79741, respectively.

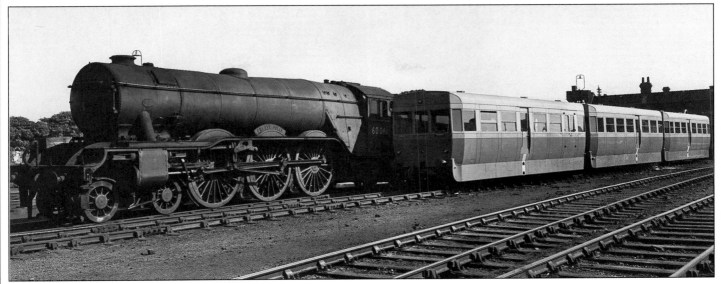

On shed at Neasden in 1952, the first unit looks rather flimsy in comparison with Gresley 'A3' class Pacific No 60061 *Pretty Polly*.

On 26 May 1952, just three days after being introduced to the press, the new train is seen at the buffer-stops at Marylebone station. Formed of two power cars and a trailer, the unit provided a total seating capacity for 129 passengers, 32 in the driving motor third class brake, 45 in the driving motor third class and 52 in the trailer. *R. K. Kirkland*

With driving motor No 2 facing the camera, the 'ACV Demonstration Train' is seen at Harrow & Wealdstone on 14 April 1954, during a period when it operated the short branch to Belmont, which closed ten years later. Although it operated in days when a red tail lamp was still required, the unit was fitted with a modern-day two-tone air horn, described by a contemporary report as sounding like a 'raucous cuckoo call'. *C. R. Lewis Coles*

In August 1953, evaluation trials were still under way, and the first unit is pictured in Platform 5 at Birmingham Snow Hill. *Ian Allan Library*

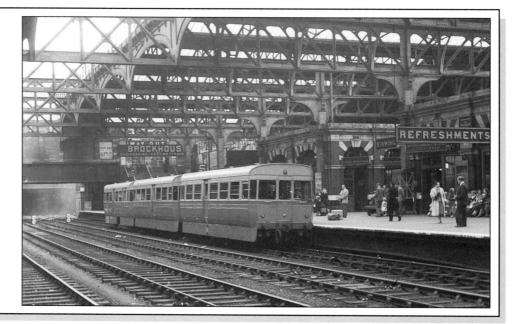

The two new BUT units commissioned by BR were painted in lined green and had the skirting panels omitted and the drop windows replaced with quarter-lights. With DMT No M79745 leading, the pristine train is posed for the official camera, when probably new from works in 1955. *Ian Allan Library*

Steam age diesel. Led by DMBS (ex-DMBT) No M79744, the second of the new BUT lightweight DMUs departs from Watford Junction, past Watford No 3 signalbox and the steam shed, heading for St Albans Abbey on 25 May 1957. The rear car, however, is from the prototype train, still having drop windows. Now painted in BR green, this vehicle also sports a grey roof. The exhaust pipe has been taken vertically upwards at the cab end. *C. R. Lewis Coles*

The bus-style seating in the Bristol/ECW railbus, which provided for 56 second class passengers. *Ian Allan Library*

With the valence containing the headlight actually concealing the unit underframe, Bristol/ECW railbus No Sc79959 is seen at Strathaven Central on 20 May 1960, working the 10.15 service for Hamilton Central. Trains ceased to operate on this line in October 1965. *John N. Faulkner*

The layout of the driving cab and control panel of Bristol/ECW railbus No Sc79958 is similar in most respects to those of the other railbus manufacturers, although individual designs for the desk and instrumentation varied quite considerably. The handle on the left is the main throttle control, and the three knobbed levers in the centre are the forward/reverse lever, the brake controller and the horn, respectively.
Colin J. Marsden collection

Waggon und Maschinenbau single-car Railbus

Built by:	Waggon und Maschinenbau
Introduced:	April 1958
Coupling Code:	None
Engine:	Buessing six-cylinder horizontal type 150hp
Transmission:	Mechanical, Cardan shaft to ZF electro-magnetic six-speed gearbox
Body:	41ft 10ins x 8ft 85/16in
Weight:	15 tons
Operating numbers:	79960 to 79964

A large number of four-wheel railbuses operated in Germany in the 1950s, and their design had become highly standardised. The Waggon und Machinenbau Company of Donauworth adapted this design to meet specifications for the BR order to provide railbuses for the UK, but nevertheless a considerable number of Deutsche Bundesbahn parts were used in the five vehicles. In the course of heavy overhauls at both Stratford and Doncaster Works, non-availability of spare parts resulted in three of the fleet (Nos E79961, E79963 & E79964) having their original Buessing engine replaced with an AEC 150hp six-cylinder engine. At this time, they also received a dark green railcar livery and yellow front-end warning panels in place of the original attractive Malachite green with silver roof and 'speed whiskers'. Closure of most of the East Anglian branch lines that they worked, resulted in all five vehicles being placed into store at Cambridge, after which two were tried out on the NER Haltwhistle-Alston branch, and later two replaced Park Royal railbuses on the LMR Buxton-Millers Dale route. These lines also closed, and the fleet was withdrawn from service between November 1966 and April 1967. Four of the five survive, however, with two to be seen on both the North Norfolk and the Keighley & Worth Valley Railways.

Operating the Bartlow branch train, Waggon und Maschinenbau railbus No E79960 trundles along between Audley End and Saffron Walden on 8 September 1959. Passenger services on the branch were withdrawn in September 1964.
E. R. Wethersett

Each railbus was divided into two saloons separated by a central vestibule which incorporated the doors, the seating being arranged to face the driver's 'cockpit' at each end of the vehicle. The Waggon und Maschinenbau fleet seated 56 passengers in second class, 28 in each saloon.
Ian Allan Library

With mandatory rear lamp in place, railbus No E79964 awaits custom at Haverhill on 9 September 1961, forming the 10.22 train to Bartlow (reverse) and Audley End. Both Haverhill and Bartlow stations closed in March 1967. The five German-built vehicles were of particular interest at the time of their introduction as part of the new railbus fleet, as they represented the one real attempt to draw upon overseas experience in the manufacture of such vehicles. All were built completely in Germany, and shipped to the UK via the Zeebrugge-Harwich ferry. *Maurice Edwards*

The only one of the five German-built railbuses to be scrapped was No E79961, which was cut up at C. F. Booth's of Rotherham in May 1968. On 21 March 1959, the vehicle is seen at Witham, waiting to depart as the 15.42 train to Braintree. Railbuses boosted passenger receipts on the Braintree line to such an extent that they became too small to cope, and were replaced by standard two-car DMUs. Since then, the line has justified electrification. *Michael Mensing*

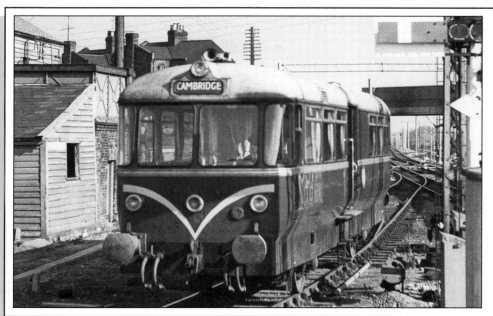

Now preserved on the Keithley & Worth Valley Railway, car No E79962 is the only one of the four survivors to retain its original Buessing engine. On 14 October 1961, it enters Marks Tey, forming the 12.56 service to Cambridge via the Colne Valley line, a route that was destined to close just ten weeks later. Observe the air horns mounted on top of the roof. *John N. Faulkner*

No E79960 awaits restoration at Sheringham, on the North Norfolk Railway, on 10 April 1977.

Beautifully restored to running order, Waggon und Maschinenbau railbus No M79964 awaits departure time at Oxenhope on 5 June 1977, forming the 10.15 Keighley & Worth Valley Railway service to Keighley.

Fully restored and operational, No E79960 works a North Norfolk Railway train from Sheringham, at Weybourne on 11 September 1983.

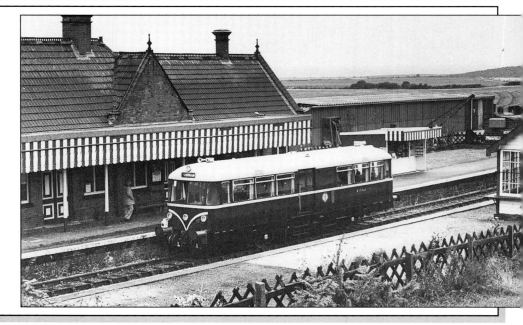

D. Wickham & Company single-car Railbus

Built by:	D. Wickham & Company
Introduced:	September 1958
Coupling Code:	None
Engine:	Meadows six-cylinder horizontal type 105hp
Transmission:	Mechanical, Freeborn-Wickham disc and ring coupling, driving Self-Changing Gears Ltd 4-speed epicyclic gearbox and cardan shaft to final drive
Body:	38ft 0in x 9ft 0in
Weight:	11 tons 5cwt
Operating numbers:	79965 to 79969

The Hertfordshire-based company of D. Wickham Ltd was well known for its tubular body construction system, in which the body was flexibly mounted upon a separate tubular underframe. The five Wickham railbuses were built to this system, leaving the underframe and bogies completely exposed to the eye. The suspension on the first four vehicles was controlled by a radius arm with semi-elliptic springs and shock absorbers, whereas the last one to be delivered, No Sc79969, had pneumatic suspension by Andre & Westinghouse,

with air bags replacing the steel springs. Unfortunately, this vehicle was the first to be withdrawn in 1963, following accident damage. The Wickham railbus fleet was the lightest of the five manufacturers and operated on Scottish Region for its relatively short life. After the premature demise of No Sc79969, two more units were withdrawn in June 1964, and the final pair succumbed to the breaker's torch in October/November 1966. None have survived into preservation.

Posed for the official manufacturer's photographs, the first Wickham railbus emerges from its factory in Ware, Hertfordshire, in the summer of 1958. No Sc79965 is painted in malachite green with yellow lining, 'speed whiskers', and has a grey roof edged with a black band. In addition to three marker lights, there is also a powerful headlight centrally placed beneath the cab windows. *Ian Allan Library*

The smart leather-trimmed upholstery of a Wickham railbus seated 44 passengers in second class. *Ian Allan Library*

Illustrating the unusual sprung metal bands fitted as dumb buffers, Wickham railbus No Sc79968 waits to depart from Crieff for Gleneagles on 23 July 1959. Passenger services ceased on this line in July 1964. *R. Furness*

With early winter snow already coating the mountains in the background, an unidentified Wickham railbus operates the Craigendoran-Arrochar & Tarbet service on a cold but sunny 9 November 1959, and displaying a rear tail lamp, approaches Glen Douglas station. The railbuses replaced steam-operated 'push-pull' trains on this service. *British Rail*

Another Wickham vehicle constructed for BR at the same time as the five railbuses was the 'Elliott High Speed Track Recording Coach', which had similarly designed bodywork to the railbus passenger fleet, but was mounted on a more substantial underframe and had proper buffers fitted. Originally liveried in brown and yellow and then in overall green, it is today in standard 'Derby Research' blue and red and is self-propelled as Departmental No (RDB)999507.

Park Royal single-car Railbus

Built by:	Park Royal Vehicles
Introduced:	July 1958
Coupling Code:	None
Engine:	BUT (AEC) six-cylinder horizontal type 150hp
Transmission:	Mechanical, Standard
Body:	42ft 0in x 9ft 3in
Weight:	15 tons
Operating numbers:	79970 to 79974

Constructed with a long overhang at each end of the body, well ahead of the wheels, the five railbuses constructed by Park Royal Vehicles seated 50 passengers in second class accommodation. In the same way as the Wickham-constructed units, the underframe and bogies were completely exposed to the eye, and neither proper buffers nor drawgear were fitted, metal bands serving as dumb buffers. These railbuses, however, also had a 'towing hook' fitted for emergencies! Allocated at first to the LMR, all five were transferred to Scottish Region in 1960, where they saw out their days around Arrochar, Alloa and Ayr. Three were withdrawn in November 1966, one in March 1967, and the final example in February 1968. None have been preserved.

Park Royal railbus No Sc79971 enters Craigendoran Upper on 11 August 1960, forming a service from Arrochar. These vehicles were fitted with a two-digit train description panel and just two marker lights, a headlight being added later at roof height. *Gavin Morrison*

Soon after delivery, Park Royal No M79973 stands at Bedford Midland Road station on 16 August 1958, railbuses having taken over the Bedford-Northampton services, which were eventually withdrawn in March 1962. Alongside is Class 4F 0-6-0 No 43971 which is allocated to Bedford shed (14E). *C. J. Polkinghorne*

Having arrived from Hitchin on 7 February 1959, No M79971 stands in the old bay platform at Bedford Midland Road, waiting for the oil lamp to be transferred to the other end of the vehicle before working the return journey. It is apparent that while the driver's window is fitted with a windscreen wiper, the front passengers' window has no such luxury. *John N. Faulkner*

Now fitted with a roof headlight, a Park Royal railbus passes Ayr shed (67C) on 23 June 1961, and approaches Newton-on-Ayr, forming the 15.30 Ayr-Kilmarnock train. Surrounded by the accoutrements of the steam age railway, the little railbus takes on a very modern-looking appearance. *S. Rickard*

Still retaining original green livery, but now having a half-yellow front warning panel in place of 'speed whiskers', Park Royal railbus No Sc79970 calls at Barassie station on 14 June 1966, forming a Kilmarnock to Ayr service. Withdrawn less than nine months later, the vehicle was cut up at Ayr shed in September 1967. *Derek Cross*

AC Cars Ltd single-car Railbus

Built by:	AC Cars Ltd
Introduced:	February 1958
Coupling Code:	None
Engine:	BUT (AEC) six-cylinder horizontal type 150hp
Transmission:	Mechanical, Standard
Body:	36ft 0in x 8ft 11in
Weight:	11 tons
Operating numbers:	79975 to 79979

Although they were allocated the highest reporting numbers of the railbus fleet, the five vehicles manufactured by Associated Commercial Cars Ltd of Thames Ditton, Surrey, were the first of their type to operate on BR metals, No W79979 being tested on Western Region in February 1958, before being transferred to Scotland. Completion of the other four cars in the batch was delayed due to a fire at the works, but they went into service on Western Region later in the year based at Swindon. The railbuses worked the Kemble to Cirencester and Tetbury branches until both these services were axed in April 1964. They then operated from Bodmin and Yeovil until January 1967, after which they were transferred to Scotland to join No Sc79979. However, it was not long before the final railbus operation ceased in January 1968, and the last four railbuses (three ACs and one Park Royal) were withdrawn in the following month, actually outlived in BR service by the last few months of steam locomotive operation. Three AC cars were originally preserved, but only two remain, both on the Colne Valley Railway.

In bright malachite green livery with matching green roof, AC Cars railbus No W79977 works the 12.20 Tetbury-Kemble service on 5 August 1963, east of Tetbury. On this Bank Holiday Monday, only three of the 46 available second class seats are occupied.
Michael Mensing

An official BR photograph of the first diesel railbus to enter Scotland on 8 August 1958. Posed at Gretna Green in the days before high-visibility vests and the Health & Safety Executive, No Sc79979 is shown with Scottish Region officials of the day, including the then General Manager, James Ness, in bowler hat and rolled umbrella. The air-operated doors and steps are shown in a lowered position suitable for passengers to use at any trackside stop, or station with a shallow platform. *British Rail*

Soon after entering service in Scotland, No Sc79979 was put to work on the Gleneagles-Crieff/Comrie service, that provided seven trains a day in each direction to Crieff, of which just one each way was extended to Comrie. Both stations closed on 6 July 1964, together with the delightfully-named intermediate stops of Tullibardine, Muthill and Highlandman. The unit awaits custom at a very wet-looking Gleneagles. *Colin J. Marsden collection*

On 20 May 1960, No Sc79979 is seen operating the 14.00 Beith Town-Barrmill-Lugton train, a service that was withdrawn on Guy Fawkes Day 1962, unfortunately without fireworks of any kind from the local population. One through train a day ran from Glasgow St Enoch, but otherwise the 12 minute journey was provided with only four other trains in each direction. Despite the central headlight below the cab windows and four marker lights being fitted, the obligatory rear oil lamp still has to be used. The roof-mounted air horns were later transferred to beneath the body. *John N. Faulkner*

Photographed from the window of a Padstow-Bodmin Road train at Boscarne Junction on 13 August 1966, AC Cars railbus No W79978 waits in hope for some passengers to Bodmin North. Originally preserved on the North Yorkshire Moors Railway, this vehicle is now on the Colne Valley Railway and has been named *Premier. Rev Graham Wise*

Like the Park Royal and Wickham railbuses, the AC Cars fleet of five vehicles also had rudimentary sprung metal bands in lieu of buffers, and a small centrally-fitted drawhook for towing in the event of a failure. Showing the steps and handrails in closed position, No W79975 is seen at Yeovil Junction on 10 April 1965. *Colin L. Caddy*

Now preserved on the Colne Valley Railway, No W79976 departs Yeovil Junction on 7 August 1965, forming the shuttle service to Yeovil Town. *John N. Faulkner*

The 5xxxx series

Gloucester RC&W Company two-car Class 100

Built by:	Gloucester Railway Carriage & Wagon Company
Introduced:	May 1957
Coupling Code:	Blue Square ■
Engines in each Driving Motor:	Two BUT (AEC) six-cylinder horizontal type 150hp
Transmission:	Mechanical, Standard
Body:	57ft 6in x 9ft 3in
Weight:	DMBS 30 tons 5cwt
	DTCL 25 tons
Operating numbers:	DMBS 50339 to 50358, 51108 to 51127
	DTCL 56094 to 56113, 56300 to 56319
Renumbered:	DMBS 50351 to 53351, 50353 to 53353, 50355 to 53355;
	50356 to 53356, 50358 to 53358
	DTCL 56106 to 54106, 56108 to 54108, 56111 to 54111, 56113 to 54113

Built for general branch line and local services, 40 'semi-lightweight' twin units were produced by the Gloucester RC&W Company in 1957-8 as its version of the original two-car 'Derby Lightweights'. Use of steel in construction of the vehicles, however, meant that they were slightly heavier than the alloy-bodied Derby vehicles, but this proved to be justified as they well outlived the alloy-bodied units in everyday service. Allocated originally to London Midland and Scottish Regions, some were later transferred to Eastern Region, and although they were a successful design, no further orders were placed by BR. This was due to Derby Works abandoning its own alloy-bodied design of DMU and concentrating upon steel vehicles, which led to quantity production of new short underframe types such as Class 108. This move made the Gloucester design non-standard in terms of body construction, although it was still acceptable in respect of both engines and transmissions. The DMBS cars were given class number 100, with the DTCs becoming Class 143. The first vehicle was withdrawn damaged in 1966 and a few others became superfluous to requirements in the early 1970s. A pair of two-car units was acquired by the North Yorkshire Moors Railway in 1972, but were subsequently sold on when service patterns changed. The majority remained in use until the 1980s, with the last example, No 53355, not being taken out of service until June 1989, having worked from Neville Hill coupled with a Class 105 DMC. Five vehicles have escaped scrapping. DMBS No 50341 is on the West Somerset Railway, and DMBS No 51118 is on the Airfield Line. DTCLs

No 56097 and No 56301 are with the Mid-Norfolk Railway, and No 56317 can be seen on the Swindon & Cricklade Railway.

Approaching Edinburgh Waverley station through Princes Street Gardens on 8 August 1958, an original Gloucester twin with DMBS No Sc51112 trailing, operates a cross-city Edinburgh suburban service from Corstophine to Rosewell & Hawthornden. The latter station closed for traffic in September 1962; Corstophine survived until January 1968.

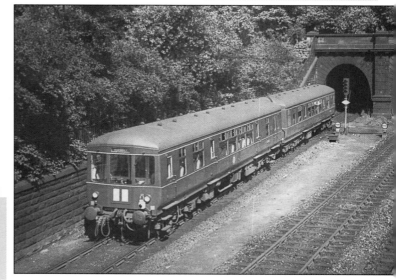

Just weeks after completion at Gloucester Works, DTCL No Sc56095 is paired with DMBS No Sc50340 for an official photograph prior to a trial run on 17 June 1957. In original lined out malachite green livery before the addition of 'speed whiskers', the vehicle is fitted with just one marker light in the cab roof and displays a two-figure route indicator in addition to a destination blind and a blue square coupling code. *Colin J. Marsden collection*

The interior of a Gloucester driving trailer composite as new. First class seating is restricted to 12, arranged in pairs, with the 54 second class mainly arranged with three seats on one side of the car with two on the other. The motor brake provided seats for 52 second class ticket holders.
Ian Allan Library

Still in original livery with a plain green front end, a Gloucester twin, with DMBS No Sc51126 leading, makes the Edinburgh Waverley stop on the main line through platforms on 22 May 1962. It forms the 13.25 train from Corstophine to North Berwick.
Michael Mensing

Operating what was then a nine-minute journey between Millers Dale and Buxton, a two-car Gloucester unit awaits departure from beneath the overall roof of the Midland station at Buxton on 23 September 1961. DMBS No M50358 now sports 'speed whiskers', and is the one driving car of the original Gloucester RC&W fleet that was experimentally fitted with CAV Ltd automatic gear change equipment.
Michael Mensing

Sporting a new half-yellow front warning panel in place of 'speed whiskers', an original Gloucester twin DMU, attached to a second generation three-car Metropolitan-Cammell unit (later Class 101), leaves Cameron Bridge for Edinburgh Waverley, forming a train from Leven. Steam still survives here in August 1965, with ex-North British Railway Class J37 0-6-0 No 64625 operating a pick-up freight consisting mainly of grain hoppers. Passenger services ceased on 6 October 1969, but the line to Cameron Bridge is currently still open for the same grain traffic. *W. J. V. Anderson*

Displaced from Scottish Region, and now attached to a Metropolitan-Cammell DMS, the same Gloucester car, DMBS No E51125, works the Alston branch service in 1968 and approaches Lambley station, having just crossed the 110ft viaduct that spans the South Tyne river. The right-hand roller blind still slips, but a new destination blind has been fitted and the number prefix 'Sc' for Scottish Region has been replaced by 'E' for Eastern Region. The Haltwhistle-Alston branch closed in May 1976. *Michael Mensing*

The 09.45 train from Harwich Town to Ipswich negotiates Manningtree Junction on 30 April 1969, formed of an original Gloucester twin, DMBS No E51115 leading driving trailer No E56307. This was also a unit originally based in Scotland that had been transferred across the border to Eastern Region. The driving motor retains green livery, but the trailer has been painted into the then new overall BR 'corporate blue'. *G. R. Mortimer*

Passing Old Philipstoun, near Linlithgow, on 29 January 1981, Class 101 DMBS No Sc51466 leads a three-car Metro-Cammell formation, diagrammed for the 10.49 Edinburgh-Glasgow Queen Street stopping train. The insignia 'TransClyde' is discernible on the bodyside.

Reversing away from Cromer terminus on 11 September 1983, the 11.40 train from Sheringham to Norwich is formed of a three-car Class 101 Metro-Cammell unit, with trailer brake No E59078 flanked by two DMCLs No E50139 and No E50191. Cromer's Midland & Great Northern Railway signalbox dates from around the early 1920s.

In contrast to Cromer, where the station retains much original charm, the end of the line at Sheringham on the same day consists of a bus shelter, a puddled car park and an uncovered platform. On arrival as the 11.40 train from Norwich, newly renumbered Class 101 DCML No E53177 (ex-E50177) is the leading vehicle of a three-car Metro-Cammell formation.

Renumbered from E50191, Class 101 DMCL No E53191 leads a three-car Metro-Cammell unit across Reedham Swing Bridge on 6 July 1985, forming the 16.26 train from Lowestoft to Norwich. Being a summer Saturday, the bridge is kept open for river traffic priority unless a train is due. *Brian Beer*

A pair of three-car Class 101 Metro-Cammell units make up a six-car excursion train from Redditch to Windsor & Eton Riverside on 28 April 1984, seen here at Staines prior to reversing to gain the Windsor branch. With the front-end window surrounds painted in black, DMCL No M53323 leads TCL No M59129, DMBS No M53307, DMCL No M53331, TCL No M59125 and DMBS No M53308.
Colin J. Marsden

A small fleet of three Class 101 two-car DMUs was allocated to Parcels Sector in 1987, but were withdrawn from service in 1989, when the Sector decided to operate only converted BR Derby Class 114s and Gloucester RC&W Class 128 Motor Parcels Vans. With a centre band of red/yellow added to the blue and grey paintwork as an interim 'Royal Mail/Express Parcels' livery, unit No E51430/51441 is stabled at Cambridge on 23 March 1987.

With a Parcels Sector BR Derby Class 114 two-car unit attached for Stamford, the 10.13 Cambridge-Peterborough mixed train passes Three Horse Shoes signalbox, near Whittlesea, on 15 July 1987, led by a Class 101 Metro-Cammell twin with DMBS No E51441 leading. Stencilled on the front is the Cambridge depot unit number '06'.

Formed of a standard DMCL/TSL/DMBS combination, immaculate Haymarket-based Metro-Cammell unit No 101318, made up of cars Nos Sc53176/59061/51244, passes Bo'ness Junction on 30 May 1988, working the 15.03 train from Stirling to Edinburgh. Scottish Region often used the class number in this way on its DMUs as part of the unit identity, although the practice was at first inconsistent.

Consisting of Metro-Cammell Class 101 DMBS No 53155 and newly corridor-connected Pressed Steel Company Class 121 DTS No 54287, a hybrid unit for working Network SouthEast(NSE) 'Thames' branches, stands inside Old Oak Common depot on 27 November 1988. Newly painted in NSE red, white and blue colours, it displays a new unit number (L)206.

Given Plymouth Laira unit number P861, Class 101 motor brake No 53157 and Gloucester RC&W Class 122 'bubblecar' No 55012, work the 10.12 Paignton to Exmouth train on 13 January 1989, passing Aller Junction, near Newton Abbot. Unlike the hybrid unit in the previous illustration, this one is not gangway connected.

Displaying the Class number '101' on the front end, with NSE branding, a Metro-Cammell DTCL No 54358 forms a hybrid two-car unit with BR Derby Class 108 DMBS No 51942. The liveries match well, but the special white roof treatment given to the driving trailer and the removal of roof air vents contrasts with the standard dark grey, air-vented roof of the motor brake. The train is climbing to Sharnbrook summit, south of Wellingborough, on 11 March 1989, and forms the 11.23 train from Bedford to Kettering.

As the first generation DMU fleets grew older and older, instances of hybrid vehicle formations naturally became more commonplace due to driving motor failures. On 22 June 1991, Metro-Cammell Class 101 DMBS No 51225 of set L202, leads Pressed Steel Company Class 117 TCL No 59514 and DMS No 51404, both cars from unit No L424. The 'L' prefix to the unit number stands for 'London', it being allocated to Reading for operating local services between there and Paddington. The same prefix was used for units allocated to Old Oak Common. The train approaches Twyford as the 12.42 from Paddington to Reading.

Regional Railways Sector cosmetically refurbished the interiors of a number of its Metro-Cammell Class 101 units allocated to both Norwich and Longsight Depots, and at the same time applied its own original livery of dark blue/light blue and grey. The '101' class number, with the set number is shown on the front end. On 1 August 1992, DMBS No 51428 and DTCL No 54062 forming unit No 101655, approach Reedham Junction, working a Norwich-Lowestoft train. A now mandatory headlight is fitted centrally between the marker lights.

Running alongside the New Cut, where it joins with the River Waveney at Haddiscoe, the 17.40 train from Lowestoft to Norwich on 15 August 1992 is formed of Metro-Cammell unit No 101660. This consists of DTCL No 54343 leading DMBS No 51189. Following attention to the roof covering, the usual ventilators have been dispensed with.

Withdrawn from revenue-earning service in 1989, Metro-Cammell DMBS No 53222 and DTCL No 53338 were converted for Derby Railway Technical Centre use and became Departmental vehicles RDB977693 and RDB977694, respectively. Standing in the RTC Research yard, the unit is the first to be painted into a new Research two-tone grey livery with 'Laboratory 19' and the thin band below the windows both in red. Following on from *Test Car Iris*, the set was dubbed *Iris II*. *Colin J. Marsden*

Numbered DB977392, Metro-Cammell Class 101 DMS No 53167 was one of two such vehicles transferred to Departmental stock and rebuilt at Cardiff Cathays as 'Ultrasonic Test Coaches' for the Director of Civil Engineering. Leading the train through Whifflet station on 15 October 1993, the centre vehicle is Instrumentation Coach No DB999602 and the rear vehicle is No DB977391 (ex-Class 101 No 51433). The unit is now owned by Serco and is currently painted in the company colours of red and grey.

In striking Strathclyde PTE orange and black livery, a Glasgow Corkerhill-based Metro-Cammell Class 101 power twin No 101693 arrives at its destination of Whifflet on 15 October 1993, forming the 12.43 train from Glasgow Central. DMSL No 53266 leads DMBS No 51192.

Formed of DMBS No 51187 and DMSL No 51509, Metro-Cammell 'power twin' No 101684 awaits departure from Glasgow Central on 2 May 1995, forming the 15.13 train for Whifflet. The new 'ScotRail' emblem introduced in 1995, can be seen on the bodyside and on the front end. In Platform 4, a second-generation DMU, Class 156 'Sprinter' No 156476, forms the 15.10 train for East Kilbride.

The only three-car Metro-Cammell unit in the colours of Regional Railways, set No 101683, pauses for the Dolwyddelan stop on 18 August 1994, forming the 09.37 train from Blaenau Ffestiniog to Llandudno. Formed of two driving motors with a trailer second No 59303 between, both the leading brake No 51177 and the trailing vehicle No 53269 are fitted with 'train to shore' radio transmission equipment, the fitting for which can be clearly seen from this angle, in the roof above the driving cab. *Brian Beer*

Fairly ancient and fairly modern: repainted to original green livery with a half-yellow front panel, Longsight-based three-car Metro-Cammell unit No 101685 awaits departure time at Chester on Christmas Eve 1994, forming the 11.23 service to Llandudno Junction. DMSL and DMBS cars No 53160 and 53164 power the unit at each end of TSL No 59539. In the opposite platform, Class 158/0 No 158752 forms the 09.56 'Regional Express' from Llandudno to Manchester Piccadilly. *Ken Brunt*

Class 101 DMBS vehicles No 53200 and 53231 have been converted into a Class 960 'Sandite' unit based at Longsight, No 960994. Stabled in the holding bay at Liverpool Lime Street station on 11 June 1994, the individual cars now carry Departmental numbers 977901 and 977902, respectively. *Chris Dixon*

Approaching its destination on 1 March 1991, the 10.35 Reading-Gatwick Airport Service is formed of three-car Metro-Cammell Class 101 unit No L837. Leading is DMBS No 51437, one of the vehicles constructed to seat 52 second/standard passengers but specially modified for this service with extra luggage racks, reducing seating capacity to 49.

Soon after transfer from Norwich Depot to Longsight, and retaining NSE livery, Metro-Cammell 'power twin' No 841 crosses the River Glaze at Glazebrook on 25 February 1994, formed of DMCL No 53332 and DMBS No 53312. The train is working over the ex-Cheshire Lines Committee main line, diagrammed for the 11.13 service from Wilmslow to Warrington Central. *Chris Dixon*

Modified for the Reading-Gatwick Airport services, with some seats removed and additional luggage racks fitted, Class 101 set No L840 departs from Manchester Oxford Road station on 24 November 1995. Now transferred to Longsight depot, DMBS No 53311 and DMC No 53322 form empty stock from the 10.44 Irlam-Oxford Road service.

On a bitterly cold day in Glasgow, with snow in the air, Metro-Cammell '101' 'power twin' No 101692 soldiers on in service, arriving at Central station as the 09.06 train from Whifflet on 26 January 1996. Although the two driving motors, Nos 53170 and 53253, were first introduced in traffic in 1957, a replacement on Strathclyde services is unlikely to arrive until ScotRail's 'third generation' 'Turbostar' Class 170/4 DMUs are delivered from Adtranz, Derby, in Millennium year 2000.

Converted for use as an observation saloon for the Kyle of Lochalsh line in 1986, Class 101 driving trailer No 54356 was renumbered 6300 as hauled coaching stock. Provided with locomotive-compatible electrics, the vehicle had partitions removed, carpets fitted, random seating provided and a public address system installed. Originally left in blue/grey livery, it was later repainted green and white, and named *Hebridean*. Introduction of Class 156 'Sprinters' on West Highland services made the car redundant, and on 28 February 1996, it was looking sorry for itself on depot at Inverness. Currently, the vehicle is a subject for preservation, and has been moved to the Gloucestershire Warwickshire Railway at Toddington.

Repainted under contract to the newly-created Strathclyde Transport Authority, Class 101 'power twin' unit No 101692 in Caledonian blue livery, arrives at Motherwell on 15 September 1997, forming the 13.08 train from Cumbernauld. Consisting of DMSL No 53170 and DMBS No 53253, the unit is normally dedicated to the Cumbernauld services. The new ScotRail logo is evident on the driver's cab door.

Now operating as a two-car 'power twin' without a set number, green-liveried Class 101 driving motors Nos 53164 and 53160 depart from Manchester Piccadilly station on 27 October 1997, forming the 10.46 service to Sheffield. It is conceivable that this unit could remain in service with North Western Trains until its new 'Juniper' DMUs, ordered from GEC Alsthom, commence service in the year 2000.

Diesel multiple-units converted for 'Sandite' application use are now owned by Railtrack plc. Two of them, sets Nos 960994 and 960991, in blue/grey and NSE colours, respectively, are seen parked in the single siding behind platform 1 at Manchester Piccadilly on 4 December 1997. *Alan Sherratt*

Park Royal two-car Class 103

Built by:	Park Royal Vehicles Ltd
Introduced:	November 1957
Coupling Code:	Blue Square ■
Engines in each Driving Motor:	Two BUT (AEC) six-cylinder horizontal type 150hp
Transmission:	Mechanical, Standard
Body:	DMBSL 33 tons 8cwt
	DTCL 26 tons 7cwt
Operating numbers:	DMBSL 50395 to 50414
	DTCL 56150 to 56169

Although known principally as road vehicle coachbuilders, the North London-based Park Royal Vehicle Company pioneered the GWR railcars in association with AEC Motors, constructing the bodywork for the first four, and in 1952 also built the 11 BUT Railbuses already described, in addition to units for Ireland. Having this experience, the company naturally tendered for the construction of at least some of the large number of new vehicles required under the BR Modernisation Plan. It was successful in obtaining a contract for 20 two-car units designed to 1955 BR specifications and powered by AEC engines. In appearance these closely followed the style of the 'Derby Lightweights', but they had a number of detail differences and were quite distinctive in appearance. In the late 1960s, the driving motor vehicles were classified 103 and the driving trailers became Class 145. Constructed with both light alloy and steel with riveted joints, engine vibration was a major factor in the bodywork becoming troublesome. The fleet was omitted from the BR DMU refurbishment scheme, and the first withdrawals from traffic commenced in the early 1970s, with the final car taken out of BR service in February 1983. Initially a number of vehicles escaped breaking up, being taken into preservation or transferred for Departmental use. Of these, four cars currently survive, Nos 50413 and 56169 on the West Somerset Railway and Nos 50397/56160 on the Mid-Norfolk line.

The first class section of the Park Royal Driving Trailer Composite vehicles provided for 12 seats in three bays, with another 48 seats available as second class. *Ian Allan Library*

Brand-new from works in April 1958, DMBS No M50400 is matched with DTCL No M56155, to work a special train for test purposes and for photographs to be taken. In original Brunswick green livery with cream lining, grey roof and prominent red bufferbeam, 'speed whiskers' were to come later. The Park Royal design with rounded roof and windows was attractive, and the provision of both a destination panel below the cab roof and a two-figure headcode box did not detract. Note the blue square coupling code beneath the two marker lights. *Ian Allan Library*

Despite having standard engines and transmissions, with the 'blue square' coupling code enabling them to be used with units of different manufacture, the 20 Park Royal twins were considered as non-standard. They were nearly always associated with London Midland Region services from Chester to Wales and the West Midlands. On 2 July 1960, however, DMBS No W50414 and DTCL No W56168 strayed on to the Belmont branch, from where they pass Headstone Lane, returning to Watford Junction as an empty coaching stock working. 'Speed whiskers' are now apparent. *John N. Faulkner*

Specifications laid down to the manufacturers of the first generation diesel railcars resulted in the nearest thing then seen to a standard driving cab. The driving position was always on the left side in the direction of travel, and the cab was designed for one person operation, a non-driving seat being provided for route training and the like. Although different styling was adopted by the various manufacturers, all were obliged to follow a common theme, with the driver's left hand controlling the throttle handle and the right hand operating the four-position gear selector, direction lever and vacuum brake valve. The desk dials included gauges for rpm, speed, vacuum brake and brake cylinder pressure, and the switches activated the screen de-mister and lit up the panel lights and the headcode and route indicator panels. Provision was made between the switches for the driver's master key, and on the non-driving side of the cab was a handbrake wheel for applying a parking brake to the bogie beneath it, an emergency brake valve and the train lighting and heating switch panel. On the left-hand wall between the cab door and front windows, the engine control panel was situated, enabling units working in multiple to be operated from the front cab. This Park Royal driving cab conforms reasonably to the standard layout specifications, although the lighting control switch has been placed above the gear selector. *Colin J. Marsden collection*

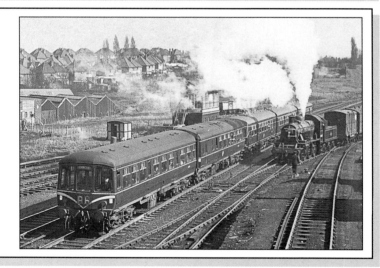

Formed of a Park Royal twin and a three-car Metro-Cammell unit, the 12.15 train from Coventry to Birmingham New Street approaches Stechford on 17 March 1962, with Park Royal driving trailer No M56159 leading. As well as 'speed whiskers', overhead electrification warning stickers are also apparent. The train is passing Ivatt Mogul No 46427, which is engaged in shunting. *Michael Mensing*

Providing second class seating for 48 passengers and 16 for any first class ticket holders, Park Royal driving trailer composite No M56163 is formed at the rear of an arrival at Pwllheli in June 1966. Retaining original green livery, the unit now carries a half-yellow front-end warning panel in addition to the then mandatory oil-fired tail lamp. *Stanley Creer*

On 17 September 1966, the 17.35 local service from Lapworth to Birmingham Snow Hill passes Bentley Heath crossing, near Knowle & Dorridge, formed of a Park Royal twin with the driving motor brake leading. This is a particularly early example of the application of all-over BR 'corporate blue' livery with the then new BR emblem. The vehicle retains a half-yellow warning panel. *Michael Mensing*

With an all-yellow front end, a Park Royal Class 103 twin accelerates away from the Colwyn Bay stop on 24 July 1973, working the 16.30 train from Bangor to Chester. *A. Wyn Hobson*

With the requirement for headcodes having ceased, the front panels of this Class 103 twin at Crewe have been blanked off. The unit forms the 13.20 for Shrewsbury on 29 August 1978. *A. Wyn Hobson*

Now downgraded from a composite vehicle, Park Royal driving trailer second No M56155 leads a five-car Class 103/101 combination on 15 September 1981, forming the 08.30 service from Llandudno to Manchester Victoria. The units are passing between Chester No 4 signal box and Chester depot, where three other Metro-Cammell DMUs are visible together with a Gloucester RC&W Class 128 Parcels car.

Passing a stabled BR Swindon Class 120 DMU in blue/grey 'InterCity' livery, DTSL No 56159 and DMBS No 50399 make up a Class 103 Park Royal twin, which is changing platforms before departing as the 10.42 from Shrewsbury to Pwllheli. With the overall roof long gone and the trackwork 'rationalised', the Shrewsbury station area is hardly recognisable from earlier days.

Although Wolverhampton Low Level station closed in 1972, the legend 'Wolverhampton High Level' is still displayed in the old destination roller blind of Class 103 DMBS No M50402, near Wellington (Salop) on 12 September 1981. The Park Royal twin leads a hybrid unit that includes Metro-Cammell Class 101 and BR Swindon Class 120 vehicles, both of which are painted blue/grey after refurbishment. The train is the 07.37 from Pwllheli to Wolverhampton.

A mixed Park Royal Class 103/BR Derby Class 108 combination departs from Chester, passing No 2 signalbox on 19 September 1981. Rostered for a Chester to Manchester Oxford Road service, DTSL No M56165 is leading.

Withdrawn from passenger duties in 1970, Park Royal DMBS No M50396 and DTSL No 56162 were converted to 'Laboratory Coach No 5' for use by the BR Research Division at Derby as a track recording unit, and the vehicles renumbered ADB975089/90. The former Motor Brake was fitted with a generator in the luggage compartment, and underfloor monitoring equipment was carried beneath both vehicles. In this guise, the life of the unit was extended until the late 1980s when it was finally withdrawn due to asbestos contamination and cut up at Mayer Newman, Snailwell, in February 1991. In red and blue Derby Research livery, 'Laboratory No 5' passes Wennington Junction signalbox on 24 November 1983. Driving trailer No RDB975090 is leading. *David Wilcock*

Carrying the words 'Instrumentation Development Section — Research & Development Division Derby' on the side, motor brake No RDB975089 leads 'Laboratory Coach No 5' passing Earls Court on 30 April 1986. Heading west, the unit is on hire to London Transport for tests on the District Line. The legend on the front below the driver's window reads 'Scientific Instruments. Must be handled with Care. Must not be Loose Shunted. Ensure Handbrakes are off before Moving'. As the unit is no longer in passenger service, the roof ventilators have been removed and covered over. *Brian Beer*

In the early days of preservation on the West Somerset Railway at Minehead, Class 6400 0-6-0PT No 6412 is about to depart with a train for Blue Anchor on 11 July 1976, while a preserved Class 103 Park Royal twin is on view in the opposite platform. Painted into green and cream livery and provided with set No P200, the unit consists of DMBS No 50413 and DTSL No 56169.

Birmingham RC&W Company two-, three- or four-car Class 104

Built by:	Birmingham Railway Carriage & Wagon Company
Introduced:	April 1957
Coupling Code:	Blue Square ■
Engines in each Driving Motor:	Two BUT (Leyland) six-cylinder horizontal type 150hp
Transmission:	Mechanical, Standard
Body:	57ft 6in x 9ft 3in
Weight:	DMBS/DMCL 31 tons
	DTCL/TSL 24 tons
	TBSL 25 tons
Operating numbers:	DMBS 50420 to 50423, 50428 to 50479, 50532 to 50541, 50594 to 50598
	DMCL 50424 to 50427, 50480 to 50531, 50542 to 50593
	DTCL 56175 to 56189
	TSL 59188 to 59208, 59230 to 59234
	TBSL 59209 to 59229, 59240 to 59244
Renumbered:	All surviving cars in both 50xxx & 56xxx series renumbered to 53xxx and 54xxx respectively in 1980-1 except 50446 and 50521, renumbered to 78851 and 78601.

After Metro-Cammell of Washwood Heath, the next largest private producer of DMU railcars for BR was BRC&W of Smethwick, Staffs, the company turning out a total of 437 vehicles of Classes 104, 110 and 118, of which 269 were power cars. The first vehicles were produced for general branch line and local services and totalled exactly 300 cars, becoming Class 104. However, the first classifications applied were as follows:

104/1	Driving Motor Composite/Second with lavatory
104/2	Driving Motor Brake Second
140	Driving Trailer Composite with lavatory
160	Trailer Second with lavatory — seating 69, or 66 if a luggage rack was installed opposite lavatory
166	Trailer Brake Second with lavatory — seating 51
169	Trailer Composite/Second with lavatory — seating 68 2nd class or 12 1st class & 54 2nd class

The BRC&W Class 104 units were a successful low density build, the last examples surviving into the 1990s, despite not being part of the 1970s refurbishment programme. They were constructed with short underframes with steel bodies of all welded construction, and had fibre glass mouldings for the roof ends of the driving compartments. The BRC&W front-end design was immediately recognisable by the three large cab windows, the tops of which were pitched above the level of the bodyside windows at cant-rail height. This feature gave a distinctive appearance to the cream lining bands, both of which had to be raised at the front corners. Two driving cars had one engine removed on an experimental basis in 1982, and together with a few vehicles attached to Scottish Region and the London area, were the only examples of the build to receive blue/grey livery. The remainder began life in original Brunswick green, and later received the then standard overall blue, with a few of the last examples being repainted into the red, white and blue colours of Network SouthEast. A total of 12 cars currently survive in preservation, principally on the Churnet Valley and Llangollen Railways, and with the Cambrian Railways Society.

Having been in traffic for a few months only, a Birmingham RC&W three-car unit departs from Stafford on 11 August 1958, forming the 14.35 train for Birmingham New Street. The vehicles are in original livery without 'speed whiskers' and are equipped with both a route indicator panel in the roof above the cab windows and a two-character headcode box beneath them.

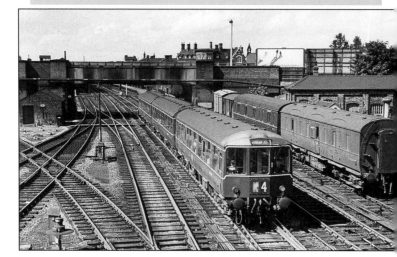

An official photograph dated 22 October 1957 shows two newly-delivered BRC&W railcar units at the new Stoke-on-Trent diesel depot in Cockshute sidings. The depot staff had custom-built facilities for cleaning and servicing up to 38 units daily, and were also equipped to tackle heavy maintenance. Both driving vehicles are fitted with a single rooftop light above the destination blind, in place of the two lights above each buffer as shown in the previous illustration.
British Rail

With driving trailer composite No E56178 leading, a four-car BRC&W unit departs from York on 21 May 1959, forming a service for Harrogate. Front-end 'speed whiskers' have been added to the original all-green livery, and the letters 'YK SET' beside each marker light represent an early example of displaying a depot allocation. The DTCL vehicles were later designated Class 140, and provided for 12 first and 54 second-class seats.

A hybrid unit formed of both BRC&W and Metro-Cammell vehicles makes a special stop at Birstworth station on 12 March 1964, forming a school special from Pateley Bridge to Harrogate. Top left of the new half-yellow warning panel, the front-end ventilation grille fitted to all BRC&W driving cars is now particularly visible against the yellow paint. Although the Pateley Bridge line closed to scheduled passenger services in April 1951, it stayed open for goods traffic until October 1964. *Gavin Morrison*

With a Class 104/2 driving motor brake facing the camera, a BRC&W three-car DMU accelerates away from Buxton on 1 May 1974, forming the 16.17 train to Manchester Piccadilly. Waiting to enter the station, another similar unit forms an empty stock working from Whaley Bridge, and will operate the next departure from Buxton to Manchester. Both units now have overall yellow fronts, but the departing one also sports white paint on the front curved roof section. *Philip D. Hawkins, FGRA*

Hauling a planked construction parcels van approaching Thurston, a three-car Class 104 unit works the 18.25 Sunday 'paytrain' service from Cambridge to Ipswich on 3 June 1979. This is believed to have been the last remaining DMU service to convey a tail load. *John C. Baker*

With Class 104/1 DMCL No M50495 leading, a three-car BRC&W unit departs from Norwich station and heads for the carriage sidings on 25 June 1975, having earlier arrived as a service from Birmingham New Street. The yellow line at cant-rail level above the first two bodyside windows indicates the position of first class seating.

On 22 September 1976, Class 104/1 driving motor composite No M50527 leads a three-car BRC&W unit approaching Manchester Victoria as empty stock from Red Bank sidings to form a service for Blackpool North. At this time, members of the class regularly performing the Blackpool diagrams were given a white band below the bodyside windows.

With the top of Blackpool Tower looming up behind Blackpool North station building, another BRC&W Class 104 'Blackpool' unit awaits the 'off' on 31 May 1980, forming the 16.20 Saturdays-only train for Manchester Victoria. The leading car, Class 104/2 DMBS No M50471, no longer has a headcode panel. From 1977 onwards, these were removed from vehicles as they passed through works and, in this case, a new centre front panel has been welded in.

Both ends of BRC&W Class 169 Trailer Composite No M59169, viewed at Blackpool North station on 31 May 1980. Unusually, very large windows were fitted in the vestibule ends of most BRC&W vehicles of this type, allowing passengers to see through to the next car but, otherwise, not affording very much of a view. There is no window in the other end of the vehicle, however, as the frosted glass in the bodyside window indicates that this is where the toilet is situated! Above the centre of the bogies at each end can be seen the lifting points, where the vehicle can be raised clear of its bogies by a works or rail-mounted crane.

Formed of two Class 104 driving motors, a BRC&W 'power twin' awaits departure from Manchester Victoria as the 14.03 to Nottingham on 25 March 1983. Vehicle No M53528, nearest to the Class 25, was previously numbered M50528, but the leading car, No M50524, still retains its original number and the 'Blackpool' body stripe.
Graham Scott-Lowe

With DMBS No M50423 leading, two three-car Class 104 units near Newton-le-Willows on 25 May 1980, form a return special from Rainhill to Manchester Victoria. One of the type fitted with a roof light instead of side lights, this motor brake also has the two-character headcode panel blinds removed and marker lights inserted. The brake compartment replaced 14 seats, the motor brakes having 52 compared with 66 in a motor second vehicle.

Disparate front-ends at the Buxton station buffer-stops on 4 September 1980. On the left, Class 104/1 DMSL No M50491 has arrived at the head of the 15.38 from Manchester Piccadilly, and displays both a roof light and marker light panel. The unit on the centre road is led by Class 104/2 DMBS No M50429, which has neither fitment, but instead has side lights and a plain front where the original headcode panel has been removed. The third car is a Gloucester RC&W Class 128 Motor Parcels Van No M55990.

Consisting of DMCL No M50508, TCL No M59164 and DMBS No M50456, a three-car BRC&W Class 104 unit sits at Rose Hill (Marple) station on 4 September 1980, having arrived as the 17.11 train from Manchester Piccadilly. It will form the 17.45 return.

A very clean three-car 104 class unit near Rotherham on 3 September 1980, forming the 17.15 train from York to Sheffield. Both driving composite cars are of a type that seat 12 first and 51 second class passengers, compared with the more usual 12 and 54, respectively.

With BRC&W Class 104 DMBS No E50596 leading Cravens Class 105 DTC No E56447, the 16.20 train to Felixstowe makes a smoky exit from Ipswich on 28 May 1981, and approaches East Suffolk Junction. Class 31/1 No 31176 awaits a favourable signal before moving a mixed freight away from the yards.

In 1982, Class 104 DMBS No M50446 and DMCL No M50521 were experimentally modified at BREL Doncaster Works with single engines developing 150bhp. Given blue/grey livery and a black strip below the front windows, the vehicles were rather amusingly reclassified as half-motor brake second, and a downgraded half-motor second, respectively. Later, it was decided to renumber all single engine cars into a 7xxxx series, and the DHMBS became No M78851 and the DHMS No M78601. The unit identification on the front of the latter vehicle is 'EXP DM352', standing for 'Experimental Diesel Mechanical 352', an indication to operating staff of the single engine modification. On 1 June 1984, the unit stands in Manchester Piccadilly, waiting to depart as the 14.50 to Rose Hill (Marple), the space on the underframe from where the second engine has been removed being discernable on both vehicles. They were both withdrawn from service in November 1985, and broken up at Cheetham Hill in September 1986.

Evoking memories of earlier days, when the front of the roof on a number of '104s' was painted white, DMBS No M53541 leads a two-car unit crossing the River Ouse, between Bedford St Johns and Bedford Midland, on 18 May 1984. The roof on both cars has been re-covered, and in the process the ventilator outlets have been dispensed with. The train is the 15.40 from Bletchley to Market Harborough. Prior to renumbering, the leading vehicle was M50541. *Tom Clift*

Allocated to Ayr Depot and painted into blue/grey livery, BRC&W three-car set No 104451 and BR Derby Class 116 three-car set No 116392 pass Prestwick airport fuel sidings on 31 May 1985, forming a service from Glasgow Central to Ayr. Renumbered from Sc50473, DMBS No Sc53473 is leading. *Rex Kennedy*

The 15.15 train from Gospel Oak to Barking approaches Upper Holloway on 15 October 1984. The BRC&W Class 104 'power twin' working the service consists of motor brake composite No E53455, and motor standard No E53522 that has had its first class seating downgraded from a motor composite. The vehicles have been renumbered from E50455 and E50522, respectively.

With silvered buffer-heads, DMBS No M53540 leads a BRC&W Class 104 twin on 19 November 1986, passing through attractive Bedfordshire countryside near Kempston Hardwick. The train is the 12.24 from Bletchley to Bedford Midland.

Replacing a failed Pressed Steel Co Class 117 power car, BRC&W Class 104 DMSL No M53520 (ex-50520) in blue/grey livery, leads a three-car hybrid unit near West Drayton on 31 May 1987. The train is the 09.42 semi-fast service from Paddington to Reading.

Near Old Oak Common on 7 September 1987, the 16.27 stopping service from Slough to Paddington, consists of a Class 104 BRC&W DMBS No M53540 (ex 50540) leading Metro-Cammell Class 101 twin No L201. The BRC&W motor brake has three front-end lights fitted, and this example has also received a Network SouthEast (NSE) branding under the centre cab window. London drivers dubbed the '104s' 'greenhouses'.

Glasgow Eastfield-allocated three-car all-blue BRC&W Class 104 DMU No (104)457 climbs Cowlairs bank as the 19.37 train from Glasgow Queen Street to Dunblane on 30 May 1988, DMSL No Sc53556 (ex-50556) leading TBSL No Sc59228 and DMSL No Sc53504 (ex-50504). Three lavatory compartments on a local short-haul service would appear something of a luxury! The two leading cars were withdrawn from traffic in May 1989 and October 1988, respectively, and No 53556 is currently preserved on the South Yorkshire Railway, at Meadowhall, near Sheffield.

With all three vehicles in NSE livery, a hybrid Class 104/101/117 three-car combination, with BRC&W DMBS No 53477 (ex-50477) leading, passes North Pole International 'Eurostar' depot on 15 March 1992. At this date, the complex is in an advanced stage of construction. The train is the 16.15 semi-fast from Paddington to Maidenhead.

Just five months prior to withdrawal, an NSE-liveried hybrid unit of Classes 104, 101 and 121 is led by Class 104 DMBS No 53539 (ex-50539) of set No L265, to form the 15.17 Paddington-Reading train. The combination rattles through Ealing Broadway on 27 July 1992, running fast from Paddington to Slough.

With 'Huddersfield' showing incongruously in the destination blind, a Llangollen Railway preserved Class 104 twin calls at Glyndyfrdwy during the 1995 Autumn Diesel Gala, leading other DMUs preserved on the line. Restored to green livery, and given a half-yellow front warning panel, motor composite No M50528 is the leading vehicle. *John Crane*

Cravens two or three-car Class 105/106

Built by:	Cravens Railway Carriage & Wagon Company (later Cravens Ltd)
Introduced:	August 1956
Coupling Code:	Blue Square ■
Engines in each Driving Motor:	Two BUT (AEC) six-cylinder horizontal type 150hp*
Transmission:	Mechanical, Standard
Body:	57ft 6in x 9ft 3in
Weight:	DMBS/DMCL 30 tons
	DTCL 23 or 24 tons
	TSL/TCL 23 tons
Operating numbers:	DMBS 50249, 50359 to 50394, 50752 to 50784,
	51254 to 51301, 51471 to 51494
	DMCL 50785 to 50817
	DTCL 56114 to 56149, 56412 to 56483
	TSL/TCL 59307 to 59325
Renumbered:	All surviving cars in both 50xxx and 56xxx series renumbered to 53xxx and 54xxx respectively in 1980-1.

* DMBS Nos 50359 to 50372 fitted with BUT (Leyland) engines and classified as 106.

Cravens of Sheffield constructed 402 passenger-carrying railcar vehicles from 1956 to 1960, of which 275 were power cars. However, the last 100 power cars to be built were provided with single Rolls-Royce engines and are described under Class 112/3. The '105' fleet was at first classified as follows:

105/1 Driving Motor Composite with BUT (AEC) engine and lavatory

105/2 Driving Motor Brake Second with BUT (AEC) engine

106 Driving Motor Brake Second with BUT (Leyland) engine

141 Driving Trailer Composite with lavatory

170 Trailer Composite/Second with lavatory

Built for general branch line and local services, the bodies of these low density units were very much on the lines of a Standard Mk1 locomotive-hauled coach, having similar side doors and windows. They were of all-steel construction, and one feature of the fabricated steel underframe was that a portion of it was designed to form the fuel tanks. In place of the more usual three front-end windows, two large ones were fitted which provided excellent forward vision for both the driver and the front seat passengers. Incorporated into the bodywork was a number of Mk1 coach features such as door droplights, window toplights and metal luggage racks, which although satisfactory in a locomotive-hauled vehicle, quickly picked up vibrations from the diesel engines and produced a distinctive and unpopular rattle. The 19 trailers constructed as composite vehicles, but soon downgraded to second class only, were all withdrawn by May 1970 as superfluous to requirements, leaving the entire fleet consisting of two-car units. Being designed for a more rural role than many actually received, all the Cravens unit vehicles had only two bodyside doors on each side of a coach, and bus-style seating. For example, the Class 106 batch were totally unsuited for the suburban duties from King's Cross that were foisted upon them following closure of the Midland & Great Northern route in 1959. Utilising three or four units coupled together for peak-time operation resulted in a great deal of empty space within the train, with up to seven driving cabs in each rake not used. With the 'Great Northern' suburban line electrified, extensive withdrawals began from the early 1980s, but a number of vehicles survived into the 1990s, and a few

even received blue/grey livery. Currently, only three cars survive in preservation, a driving trailer in service after rebuilding on the Llangollen Railway, and a two-car set on the East Lancashire Railway, transferred from its first home on the West Somerset Railway.

Looking particularly smart in Brunswick green livery, with cream 'speed whiskers' and lining and metal window surrounds, a new Cravens twin departs from Aberdeen on 11 March 1959, heading for Ballater, a line which closed to passengers in February 1966. No Sc56463, a driving trailer composite with lavatory, faces the camera and still requires the mandatory tail lamp in position. *Colin J. Marsden collection*

Not long after entering service from new, a Cravens unit restarts from North Wootton station on 3 January 1959, forming a Hunstanton–King's Lynn train. Services on the Hunstanton branch ceased on 5 May 1969, one of the many closures around this period that brought about transfer of these units to duties unfitting. The leading driving trailer has two marker lights, the blue square coupling code, a destination panel and two-character headcode box. *Rodney Lissenden*

Cravens and BR Derby units (later Classes 105 and 108) under maintenance inside the custom-built diesel depot at Allerton. *British Rail*

With front-end 'speed whiskers' replaced with a half-yellow warning panel, a Cravens twin picks up speed after the Thurston stop, working a Cambridge to Ipswich local service in 1963. The motor brake is leading. *John C. Baker*

The cab layout of a Class 105 Cravens driving car:
1. Control for four engines and indication equipment (later modified)
2. Air control pressure gauge
3. Vacuum train pipe and cylinder pressure gauge
4. Brake valve
5. Gear selector
6. Speedometer
7. Lighting control panel
8. Engine rev indicator
9. Throttle handle. *Colin J. Marsden collection*

The interior of a Cravens driving trailer composite vehicle, looking towards the first class compartment and the driving cab. In this vehicle, only first class ticket holders are privileged to have both floor carpet and a forward view through the driving windows. The backs of the three-plus-two bus-style seating in second class all contain ashtrays. *John Glover*

Formed of a Cravens twin, an off-peak stopping train from King's Cross to Welwyn Garden City climbs away from the London terminus on 22 March 1972, and is seen at Belle Isle, the name given to the short stretch of line between Gasworks and Copenhagen tunnels. Now painted in BR 'corporate blue' with a full-yellow front end, the vehicle still retains both a destination blind and headcode panel at this stage, but the ventilation panel beneath the headcode box has been plated over to make the driving cab a little more draught-proof. The roof 'studs' are also ventilators, designed to let out stale air and tobacco smoke from the passenger compartments without letting rain in.

Prior to the use of headcode panels being decreed, early build Cravens driving cars were provided with four marker lights, three below the driving cab and one in the roof. All four were still apparent on DMBS No E50369 on 7 August 1973, as the unit awaits departure from Upminster as the 15.30 train for Romford. The plate beneath the centre light is another example of the ventilator being blanked out.

In ex-works condition, a Cravens twin approaches Great Yarmouth on 8 October 1978, forming the 15.37 train from Norwich. With headcode panel removed, but retaining the front grille, Class 105/2 DMBS No E51293 leads Class 141 DTCL No E56123.

With DTCL No E56454 at the rear, three Class 106/141 Cravens twins depart from King's Cross (York Road) on 23 July 1975, coupled together to form a local service from Welwyn Garden City to Moorgate. Departing from the King's Cross main line platforms, Class 31/1 No 31218 heads an evening commuter train for Hitchin.
Graham Scott-Lowe

Forming the 15.45 train from Great Yarmouth, a hybrid two-car DMU approaches its Norwich destination on 25 June 1975. The Cravens Class 106 DMBS No E50364 leading is one of the first batch of vehicles constructed in 1956, and is fitted with four front lights including a roof light. The second vehicle is a Metro-Cammell Class 144 driving trailer composite No E56052.

Although the sun was shining on this December day in 1975, it was far from warm, so why all the window toplights are open in this Cravens twin is unknown. With Class 141 DTCL No E56417 leading, the 12.24 Saturday service from Broad Street to Welwyn Garden City emerges from Potters Bar tunnel. Overhead catenary for electrification is already in position on this stretch of line.

A King's Cross to Hitchin local service emerges from Copenhagen tunnel on 20 November 1976, led by Cravens DTCL No E56142. One of the first batch of driving trailers constructed in 1956, weighing 23 tons, these vehicles seated 12 in first class and 51 in 'second', except for five cars initially allocated to London Midland Region, which provided for 54 in second class. Apart from vehicles allocated to Scottish Region, the 1958 batch were one ton heavier.

Forming the 10.56 local service from West Monkseaton, Class 141 Cravens driving trailer No E56425 leads a Cravens driving motor into Newcastle on 4 August 1978. Having recently emerged from works overhaul, the pristine unit has first class seating downgraded and has been fitted with bars across the door windows. Its clean condition reveals the position of the warning horns beneath the buffer on the right.

With DMBS No E51286 leading, a Cravens '105' twin rounds the curve at Melton Ross, near Barnetby, on 1 September 1980, forming the 12.55 train from Cleethorpes to Doncaster. After withdrawal from service, the motor brake was one of a number of such vehicles converted for Departmental use, as either route learning cars or 'Sandite' application coaches. As a 'route learner', this example later carried number TDB977123.

To provide route training for the East Coast main line Selby diversion, four Cravens Class 105 vehicles were converted as observation saloons in 1982, and operated in pairs. With differing silver and blue roof panels, No TDB977124 and No TDB977126 are stabled at Doncaster after arrival from York. The cars were originally DMBS No 51296 and DTCL No 56445, respectively, and both were scrapped in 1990.
Colin J. Marsden

With three Metro-Cammell Class 101 units in the platforms to the rear, Cravens Class 105 DMBS No E50386 is the leading vehicle of the Cravens twin unit departing from Newcastle on 29 May 1980, and forming the 11.25 local service for Alnmouth.

A special eight-car 'Ruggex' train for Hull Kingston Rovers' supporters to watch their team play an away fixture at Leeds, departs from Hull on 31 August 1980. The train is formed of Cravens Class 105, Birmingham RC&W Class 110 and Metro-Cammell Class 101 DMUs. 23-ton Cravens driving trailer composite No E56471 leads. The first class seating, indicated by the yellow stripe above the windows, has been downgraded for the occasion.

Emerging from the southern portal of Audley End tunnel, DMBS No E51268 leads a Cravens twin, forming the 17.04 train from Cambridge to Bishop's Stortford on 1 June 1981. Although appearing to retain the small front-end grille, this has probably been plated on the inside, rather than having the usual external modification to avoid draughts.

Although the station buildings at Sudbury were still standing when this scene was photographed on 28 May 1981, they were in fact already unused and were later demolished. The 15.34 train for Colchester awaits departure, consisting of Cravens Class 105 DTCL and DMBS vehicles No E56413 and No E50383, respectively. The station has only one platform in use.

Despite not being included in the 1970s refurbishment scheme, a few of the Cravens fleet of DMUs still received blue/grey livery. This was done in order not to clash with refurbished and repainted Metro-Cammell 101 class units, with which they were regularly paired on Scottish Region. Leading two Metro-Cammell cars, a Cravens DMBS vehicle hauls the 10.14 train from Glasgow Queen Street to Edinburgh Waverley, passing Old Philipstoun, near Linlithgow, on 29 January 1981. The black marks between the front-end marker lights are where the yellow paint has chipped following minor impact damage.

Both the leading Cravens DMBS No Sc51480 and the Metro-Cammell Class 101 Driving Motor at the rear have received new blue/grey livery, but the Metro-Cammell Class 101 trailer attached has yet to be so treated. On 30 January 1981, the three-car hybrid unit departs from North Berwick branch terminus, forming the 11.05 train for Haymarket.

With a sunken boat in the picture, a Class 105 twin unit crosses Oulton Broad on 11 September 1983, forming the 09.50 train from Lowestoft to Ipswich. With first class seating still available, driving trailer No E54447 (ex E56447) leads driving motor brake No E51269. From the amount of room taken up by the brake compartment in the DMBS, it can be seen why these vehicles provided only 52 seats, nine less than a comparable driving trailer with a lavatory compartment.

In the final months prior to electrification of the line in May 1985, Class 105 twin units regularly operated services between Camden Road and North Woolwich, after which Class 313 EMUs took over, and services were extended to Richmond. With one door already flung open by an impatient passenger, the 15.58 train from Camden Road arrives at its destination on a very wet 6 April 1983, formed of DTC No E56133 leading DMBS No E50366. The stencilled 'LW' stands for 'lightweight'.

In spick-and-span condition, a Cravens Class 105 twin passes Bow Junction on 17 March 1985, on a driver route learning special. The unit is taking the line to Gas Factory Junction, which has been singled as part of the preparations for the coming of the Docklands Light Railway (DLR), and had been closed for the previous 16 months while the work was completed. The track on the right is now part of the DLR, and the signalbox has been demolished. *Ken Brunt*

One of the events of 1986 was a Cravens twin unit being returned to original lined green livery by the craftsmen of east London's Stratford Depot, under the auspices of Allan Baker. The first DMBS car delivered from the Cravens factory in August 1956, No E50359, and a DTCL No E56122 from January 1957, were rolled out at Stratford depot on 11 April 1986, and with their new numbers E53359/54122 operated a number of scheduled and special services until withdrawal in October 1988. The unit would almost certainly have been a candidate for preservation, but unfortunately the expense of removing its blue asbestos insulation was prohibitive.

A close-up of the 'Pullman-style' corridor connection between the two repainted vehicles, which also illustrates the position of the exhaust stack. The flexible pipes below the buffers are the connections for braking and train control, and the pipe running down the coach on the right is the water tank overflow from the toilet.

Two Class 105 DMBS vehicles, No E51293 and E53362, were converted to Driving Motor Parcels Vans (DMPV), and renumbered 55944 and 55945 respectively. Others of the class were stripped out and utilised on the same basis, and given an 'Express Parcels' body stripe of red and yellow, but were not renumbered. No E53365 of this batch, passes near Whittlesford on 9 July 1987, heading a four-car Parcels Sector train southwards from Cambridge. The other vehicles are a Swindon Class 120 DMBS and a two-car Metro-Cammell Class 101 unit, all similarly converted. These vehicles have 'Express Parcels' on the bodysides, but are still in blue/grey livery. *John C. Baker*

Entering Crowcombe Heathfield station on 20 August 1995, a West Somerset Railway service train from Minehead to Bishops Lydeard is formed of a preserved Cravens Class 105 DMU. Both the driving trailer No 56121 leading and the driving motor brake No 51485 have since been transferred to the East Lancashire Railway.

BR Derby three-car Class 107

Built by:	British Rail Derby Works
Introduced:	December 1960
Coupling Code:	Blue Square ■
Engines in each Driving Motor:	Two BUT (AEC) six-cylinder horizontal type 150hp
Transmission:	Mechanical, Standard
Body:	58ft 1in x 9ft 3in
Weight:	DMBS 34 tons 10cwt
	DMCL 35 tons
	TSL 28 tons
Operating numbers:	DMBS 51985 to 52010
	DMCL 52011 to 52036
	TSL 59782 to 59807

Introduced from Derby Works between December 1960 and June 1961 to work local services within Scottish Region, the 26 three-car medium-density Class 107 units are often referred to as 'Derby Heavyweights', as although constructed on a short underframe, they are considerably heavier than other similar builds from Derby, having a more robust steel construction. Before being grouped together as Class 107, the DMCL, DMBS and TSL vehicles were classified as 107/1, 107/2 and 161 respectively, the latter number shared with trailer second lavatory cars attached to Class 108 units. In 1972, it was planned to reclassify the complete Class 107 fleet as part of Class 108, but despite being reported, the change did not take place; the move was probably an error, as the two types of unit varied in many ways. After some 30 years' service, withdrawal of the fleet was completed during 1991-2, and vehicles became very popular subjects for preservation, a total of ten being currently distributed among the Caledonian, Strathspey, Eden Valley, Swindon & Cricklade and Lakeside & Haverthwaite Railways. One trailer car is also on the Battlefield Railway.

Led by DMBS No Sc51994, a nine-car formation of three low-density units constructed at Derby works for Scottish Region, pass near Pinwherry on 14 July 1962. The vehicles form the 11.03 special train from Glasgow St Enoch to Stranraer, in connection with the Saturday of the Glasgow Fair. Although the headcode panel allows for four characters, only two are being utilised. Green livery, a dark grey roof and 'speed whiskers' prevail at this time. *W. A. C. Smith*

With DMCL No Sc52033 leading, two three-car units of what was to become Class 107, call at Uplawmoor on 31 March 1962. The train is the 13.42 to Glasgow Central, the last to call at this station before it closed. Only one character shows in the headcode panel on this occasion. *W. A. C. Smith*

BR Derby two-, three- and four-car Class 108

Built by:	British Rail Derby Works	
Introduced:	May 1958	
Coupling Code:	Blue Square ■	
Engines in each Driving Motor:	Two BUT (Leyland) six-cylinder horizontal type 150hp	
Transmission:	Mechanical, Standard	
Body:	57ft 6in x 9ft 2in	
Weight:	DMBS	29 tons
	DMCL	28 tons
	DTCL	21 tons or 22 tons*
	TSL	22 tons or 22 tons 10cwt*
	TBSL	23 tons
Operating numbers:	DMBS	50599 to 50629, 50924 to 50935, 50938 to 50987, 51416 to 51424, 51901 to 51950
	DMCL	50630 to 50646, 51561 to 51572, 52037 to 52065
	DTCL	56190 to 56215, 56221 to 56279, 56484 to 56504
	TBSL	59245 to 59250
	TSL	59380 to 59390

All surviving cars in both 50xxx and 56xxx series renumbered to 53xxx and 54xxx respectively in 1980-1.

*Weight differences, due to some vehicles having two seats less, to provide space for a luggage rack.

Introduced from Derby Works between 1958 and 1961 for local services and general branch line work on Eastern and London Midland Regions, the individual vehicles making up Class 108 were initially given the following classifications:

108/1	Driving Motor Composite with lavatory
108/2	Driving Motor Brake Second
142	Driving Trailer Composite with lavatory
161	Trailer Second with lavatory (number shared with Class 107 TSLs)
167	Trailer Brake Second with lavatory

This large fleet totalled 333 vehicles, of which 210 were powered. They were very similar in appearance to the Class 107, but were of much lighter construction and generally regarded as the second 'Derby Lightweight' design. They had low-density seating with toilet facilities, and were gangwayed within sets of two, three or four cars. Although included in the BR refurbishment programme, a number of vehicles were subject to early withdrawal because of accident damage. The majority, however, remained in traffic until the early 1990s, with the final vehicle not taken out of traffic until October 1993. Currently well over 50 vehicles are in preservation, ranging from fully restored working examples to a number in semi-derelict condition awaiting an uncertain future. Preservation railways, sites and museums where Class 108 vehicles can still be seen include the Avon Valley, Bodmin & Wenford, Colne Valley, Dean Forest, East Anglian Railway Museum, East Kent, Gloucestershire Warwickshire, Great Central, Keighley & Worth Valley, Kent & East Sussex, Llangollen, Mid-Norfolk, Peak Rail, Northampton & Lamport, Pontypool & Blaenavon, Rutland Museum, Severn Valley, Southall, Swanage, Swansea Vale and Vale of Glamorgan.

Posed for a BR Cameraman prior to entering service on London Midland Region in February 1959, DMBS No M50629 and DTCL No M56215 are in original Brunswick green livery with cream lining, a white roof and 'speed whiskers'. The driving motor shows a roof destination panel, a two-character route indicator and two marker lights. The motor car seats 52 in second class, with the driving trailer accommodating 53 second and 12 first class passengers. *Ian Allan Library*

In BR Derby Works yard in February 1960, DMBS No M51416 awaits delivery. This later build incorporates a four-character route indicator panel in the cab roof, where the destination-blind box used to be, and the blind has been moved down to the centre cab window. Externally there is now little to differentiate between these units and the Class 107s. *Ian Allan Library*

Inside the London Midland Region depot of Allerton in 1963, two members of the maintenance staff pump oil into the system of DMBS No M50628, while another attends to the lighting/heating electrical control box. *Colin J. Marsden collection*

Formed of a driving motor composite, trailer second, and driving motor brake second, a three-car unit of what was to become Class 108, rasps away up the 1 in 43 gradient from Robin Hood's Bay on 25 June 1962, forming a morning Scarborough-Whitby-Middlesbrough service. The original livery is maintained except for a white roof, now more sensibly painted dark grey. Passenger services on this line were withdrawn in March 1965. *Peter J. Shoesmith*

The 14.22 local service from Lancaster arrives at Barrow-in-Furness on 10 June 1974, formed of Class 108/2 DMBS No M50971 and Class 142 DTCL No M56262. The unit has been re-liveried to BR 'corporate blue' with a full-yellow end, but retains both destination and headcode panels. A tail lamp is in position for the return journey.

Forming the 17.00 train for Kirkham & Wesham, a Class 108 twin awaits departure time from a wet Blackpool South on 31 May 1980, formed of DMBS No M50976 and DTCL No M56224. The headcode panel has been removed and the space plated over.

Having crossed from the lines on the right, the 13.05 local service from Whitehaven approaches Carlisle on 26 January 1980, formed of Class 142 driving trailer No M56247 and Class 108/2 driving motor brake No M50964. There is no visible evidence remaining of the headcode panel originally fitted between the marker lights, a completely new front section having been welded in. The mainstay of this traffic for many years, for the most part the '108s' have been replaced by rather less comfortable 'Pacers'.

With Class 108/2 DMBS No E50602 leading, a BR Derby twin enters Barnsley station on 10 February 1979, forming the 12.36 local service from Sheffield to Leeds. A 'LW' stencil denoting 'lightweight' is displayed on both lower corners of the front end, and the headcode panel has been plated over as a draught-proofing measure, particularly necessary in these conditions.

With Class 108/2 driving motor brake No M50964 leading, the 12.40 stopping train from Newcastle has arrived at Carlisle on 3 June 1977, and stopped alongside Class 86/0 electric locomotive No 86026, which is stabled on the centre roads with Class 85 No 85007. In this case, although the headcode panel has been plated, its frame has been retained.

The 'Rocket 150' event to celebrate the 150th anniversary of the opening of the Liverpool & Manchester Railway took place at Rainhill in May and June 1980. Coinciding with the 'grand cavalcade' of 25 May, a number of special trains operated from both Manchester and Liverpool, all being six- or eight-car DMUs 'borrowed' from a variety of depots, including Marylebone, Tyseley and Buxton. In three differing liveries, a return Rainhill-Liverpool special working passes through Kenyon Cutting, near Newton-le-Willows, formed of two two-car Class 108 sets leading a four-car Class 115. The driving vehicle, '108/2' DMBS No M51937, is refurbished in blue/grey and is followed in formation by vehicles No M56278 in white with blue stripe, all-blue Nos 56497 and 50627, blue/grey Nos 51852, 59722 and 59715, and all-blue No 51860 bringing up the rear.

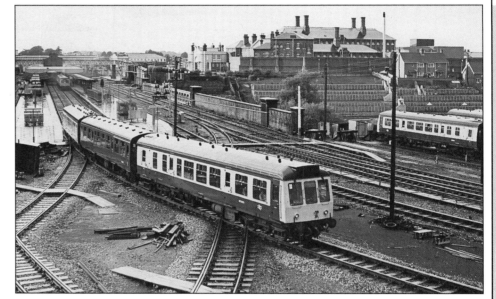

With the centre trailer composite still to be refurbished and repainted, a three-car Class 108 unit departs from Shrewsbury on 12 September 1981, forming the 17.45 stopping service to Wolverhampton. In the sidings on the right is a Metro-Cammell Class 101 unit, and in the distance is a BR Swindon Class 120 awaiting departure on a Central Wales train.

Well before the majority of reconditioned Class 108 vehicles were repainted into off-white with a blue band, it was realised that this new livery, initially intended for all DMUs in the refurbishment programme, became quickly work-stained and grubby-looking. The vehicles so treated were soon repainted, and following works' attention, the remainder of the fleet appeared in blue/grey, then the livery for InterCity trains. While in short-lived off-white/blue colours, a Class 108 BR Derby twin departs from Skipton on 24 January 1981, forming the 09.42 train for Leeds.

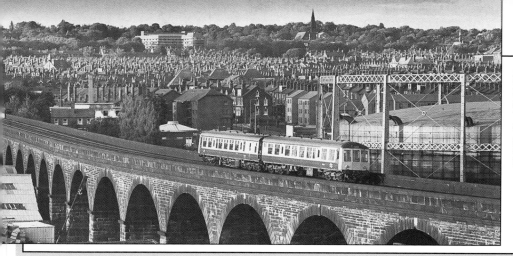

Looking smart in newly-applied blue/grey livery, a Class 108 'power twin' crosses Kirkstall viaduct on 22 August 1982, approaching Leeds with a local service from York, via Harrogate. The band at cant-rail level on the leading driving motor composite is yellow, and shows where the two first class compartments are situated. The second car is a motor brake. *David Wilcock*

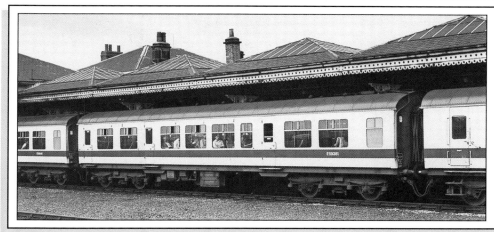

A total of 35 trailer second vehicles of this type emanated from Derby Works; the first nine constructed in 1958 were used with the Class 108 fleet, and the second batch of 26 were drafted to Scotland as centre cars for Class 107s. The only vehicles to share a classification, the complete fleet became Class 161, but when individual car classes were discontinued in favour of a general unit classification, they were merged into their respective 107 and 108 types. At Malton on 2 September 1980, car No E59381 is part of a newly-liveried four-car Class 108 unit working the 12.19 York-Scarborough train. The frosted glass window shows where the lavatory compartment is situated.

Augmented with a Metro-Cammell Class 101 centre trailer, a BR Derby Class 108 twin, with DMCL No E50643 leading, leaves Guiseley on 12 February 1983, forming the 12.57 train from Ilkley to Leeds. This line is now electrified, but due to lack of suitable modern motive power, is currently worked by Class 308 EMUs constructed in 1961! New trains were ordered by Regional Railways North East in 1998, however, and Class 333 EMUs are scheduled to be in operation on these services soon after the millennium year 2000.

Drawing into the through platforms at Altrincham, the 11.00 Manchester (London Road)-Chester train is made up of a Class 108 twin, with DTCL No M54499 leading DMBS No M51416. The driving trailer has been renumbered from M56499, to avoid conflict on the BR TOPS computer with Class 56 locomotives.

The yard lights at Buxton depot penetrate a cold mist and produce a rather unusual effect upon a three-car Class 108 unit, which has DMBS No M53932 facing the camera. In this case, it has been renumbered from M50932, so as not to clash with the Class 50 locomotive fleet. Class 20 locomotives comprise most of the other motive power that can be seen stabled here on the night of 21 February 1985.

Two Buxton-allocated three-car Class 108 DMUs, with DMCL No M52058 leading, pass Clayton Bridge on 31 August 1985, forming the 11.05 service from Llandudno to Stockport. The distinctive white cab roofs were a Buxton depot trademark. *Alan Sherratt*

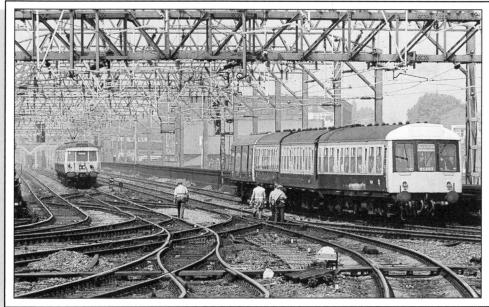

The 13.18 Manchester Piccadilly-Buxton train approaches Stockport on 4 July 1985, with a Class 303 EMU receding into the distance on a Crewe-Manchester Piccadilly working. The unusual make up of the Buxton train is Class 108 DMCL No M52021, ex-Class 107 TSL No M59794, Class 108 DMBS No M51936, and Class 128 motor parcels van No M55994 bringing up the rear. The ex-'107' trailer was the only example used with Class 108 stock, and it was returned to Ayr depot again after some two years on Buxton depot's allocation. *Paul Shannon*

Approaching Cardiff Central on 10 September 1987, to form a service for Merthyr Tydfil, a three-car Class 108 unit is headed by DMBS vehicle No W53941. Front-end embellishment includes a Welsh dragon, and the legend on the bodyside reads 'Trên y Cwm', the English translation 'Valley Train' being on the opposite side.

Looking as if its front end may have been used for target practice on a rifle range, DMBS No Sc51936 is before the camera on 29 May 1988, leading TSL No Sc59386 and DMCL No Sc52051. The three-car Class 108 set No 384 is awaiting departure from Edinburgh Waverley as the 22.15 train for Dunblane. With the trailer having 68 standard class seats, the motor brake 52, and the downgraded motor composite 53 plus 12 ex-'firsts', the unit provides for 185 seated passengers. In the adjacent platform, a Class 150/2 'Sprinter' No 150257 forms the 22.10 service for Dundee.

Still decorated on the front end with a 'Buxton Spa Line' logo, despite having been transferred from Buxton depot to Chester, Class 108 power twin No CH621 approaches Coseley on 9 April 1990, substituting for a 'Sprinter' on the 11.29 service from Birmingham New Street to Pwlhelli. With the regional letter prefix now discontinued, driving motor No 52049 leads motor brake No 51902.

Fitted with barred door windows and a now mandatory centre headlight, a Class 108 twin stands at the sole surviving bay platform at the east end of Newcastle station on 12 July 1990. Driving trailer No 54265 faces the camera, and the unit is powered by driving motor brake No 53954. A self-changing gearbox has been fitted on an experimental basis, and the legend 'Auto-Gear' is clearly displayed on the front-end, to avoid any possible confusion for drivers.
Ian S. Carr

At Sharnbrook summit, near Wellingborough, on 10 August 1988, the first Class 108 unit to be given Network SouthEast livery, forms the 14.23 train from Bedford to Kettering. The power twin comprises driving motor brakes No 53628 leading No 51942. Both vehicles are the subject of preservation, the first having been taken on by the Colne Valley Railway, and the second by the Pontypool & Blaenavon Railway.

For a time, Class 108s were the latest motive power to operate the 'Three Counties' route between Bedford and Bletchley (since rechristened the 'Marston Vale Line'), now currently in the hands of Pressed Steel Class 117 units of similar vintage. On 30 March 1990, the 15.30 Bletchley-Bedford train passes near Kempston Hardwick, and consists of NSE-liveried DTCL No 54271, being propelled by DMBS No 51909. Both vehicles have been preserved on the Avon Valley Railway.

But for 'speed whiskers' being incorporated as part of the half-yellow front warning panel, a two-car Class 108 unit was returned to original green livery in 1986, and on 19 July of that year, stands on depot at Carlisle Upperby forming the shuttle between Carlisle station and the depot for its Open Day. The two vehicles involved, DTCL No 54247 and DMBS No 53964, were later placed into regular service on the Furness Line, and both were withdrawn at the same time and cut up in 1992. *Colin J. Marsden*

Displaying a 'Liverpool St' destination blind, Class 108 DTC No M56491 stands at Chappel & Wakes Colne on 15 April 1985, attached to DMBS No M53599, which is still in NSE colours. The '108' driving trailer has been returned to its original green livery and number. Both cars are preserved on the East Anglian Railway Museum line.

The inaugural passenger train to run on the East Kent Light Railway was formed of a preserved Class 108 DMU twin, consisting of DMCL No 51572 and DTCL No 53971. On the opening day, 24 June 1995, the unit is seen with an 'Eythorne' route indicator, and also carries the special name 'The Whitecliffs Ltd' in the driving window. *Andy French*

Wickham two-car Class 109

Built by:	D. Wickham & Company
Introduced:	August 1957
Coupling Code:	Blue Square ■
Engines in each Driving Motor:	Two BUT (Leyland) six-cylinder horizontal type 150hp
Transmission:	Mechanical, Standard
Body:	57ft 0in x 8ft 3in
Weight:	DMBS 37 tons 10cwt
	DTCL 20 tons 10cwt
Operating numbers:	DMBS 50415 to 50419
	DTCL 56170 to 56174

Based at Ware, Hertfordshire, the firm of D. Wickham & Company supplied lightweight vehicles of various types to many countries around the globe. In so doing they acquired expertise in constructing bodies of a skeletal type, without the usual robust underframe associated with railway vehicles. This technique provided considerable weight saving, but in the event of even minor accident damage, was far more expensive to repair. It is likely that this was the reason why BR ordered only five two-car units from the company for service evaluation. Although quite successful, their interior design was considered by many to be rather too flamboyant and extravagant in nature. This factor together with a particularly original front-end appearance, resulted in the small fleet being considered by BR as oddities, and no further orders were placed. The units were put to work on Eastern Region, and operated branch line and local services in East Anglia. As early as September 1961, two sets consisting of vehicles Nos 50415/56170 and 50419/56174 were withdrawn from service for sale to the Trinidad Government Railway, where lightweight construction was a prerequisite for railcars. By now completely non-standard, two of the remaining three units were withdrawn in 1971, and the final set, Nos 50416/56171, was converted the following year to become the Eastern Region General Manager's Saloon, complete with kitchen facilities. Although vandalised while it was stored for a period at Stourton, Leeds, the unit has survived and is currently under restoration at the Midland Railway Centre, Butterley. After completion, it is hoped that this unique train will run again on the Llangollen Railway.

Clearly illustrating the skeletal nature of the Wickham vehicles, the framework of one during construction is recorded by an official cameraman in 1957. *Ian Allan Library*

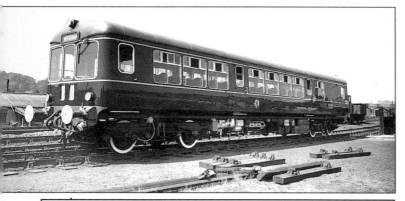

Immediately recognisable from other types of DMU introduced at the time, the first completed Wickham vehicle, DMBS No E50415, displays its bright malachite green livery with yellow lining, and clearly shows the roof cant-rail line dipped in the middle to pass beneath the roof-mounted destination panel and top marker light. The unit was displayed at the 'Modern Rail Travel Exhibition' at London's Battersea Wharf in June 1957, prior to entering BR service in August of the same year. The attendant trailer was also on view at the time, but was in an unfinished condition to show the skeletal body framework used in the manufacture. Other features at this stage included polished metal alloy window surrounds, a red bufferbeam area, painted wheel rims and three marker lights. The twin headcode panels were later flanked by 'speed whiskers'. *Colin J. Marsden collection*

A Wickham driving vehicle under construction inside the company's workshops at Ware in Hertfordshire during 1957, the framework now covered in light alloy body panels. *Ian Allan Library*

With DMBS No E50417 leading, two Wickham two-car units stand in the bay platform at Wickford on 15 December 1957, waiting to depart as the branch train for Southminster. The headcode and route indicator panels are both blank, and 'speed whiskers' have yet to be added. *Frank Church*

Part of the attractive second class interior of a Wickham driving motor brake, showing the draught-proof screens on each side of the central doors. The seat moquette is brown with green and yellow markings, and the leather is also green. The motor brake vehicles had seating for 59 in second class. The driving trailer composites accommodated 48 second class, with just 16 seats allotted for first class ticket holders. *Gordon McLeish*

Due to the different styling adopted by the various DMU manufacturers, a number of detail differences existed on individual builds, but they all followed a common theme. As with other types, the Wickham driving cab has the throttle handle controlled by the driver's left hand, with his right hand operating the gear selector and direction lever. To the extremity of his right arm is the vacuum brake valve, fitted with a removable control handle. A functional cab rather than a comfortable-looking one. *D. Wickham & Co Ltd*

Branded 'Trinidad Government' and displaying the appropriate logo, two Wickham two-car DMUs sold to the Trinidad Government Railway are seen in Trinidad shortly after their arrival, *circa* 1961. They retain 'speed whiskers', but now have a number on the bufferbeam and steps for low platforms. The Trinidad railway system closed on 28 December 1968, when services on the final section between Port of Spain and Arema were withdrawn. Last seen, some of the Wickham vehicles were being used as dwellings by poorer members of the local community! *Ian Allan Library*

Withdrawn before class numbers became widely used, the three remaining Wickham two-car units were nevertheless classified 109 for the motor brake vehicles, and 146 for the driving trailers. Prior to becoming the Eastern Region General Manager's saloon in 1972, DTCL No E56171 is propelled into Ipswich on 17 October 1964 by DMBS No E50416. The train is the 13.20 from Bury St Edmunds, and displays both route and headcode panels with a half-yellow front warning panel. The blue square coupling code is also prominent. *John N. Faulkner*

Working a Cambridge to Ipswich train, via Stowmarket, Wickham cars Nos E56172/50417 make the Elmswell stop on 23 October 1965. The original bright malachite green livery has been toned down by a liberal coating of workaday grime. *G. R. Mortimer*

Prior to the Shelford-Sudbury line closing in March 1967, services between Cambridge and Ipswich were also routed this way, via Bartlow, Haverhill, Sudbury, Colchester and Manningtree. Entering Brantham Cutting, north of Manningtree, on 4 June 1965, the 05.45 service over the route is formed of Wickham cars Nos E56173/50418. Throughout their days on BR, the five units remained in original formation. *G. R. Mortimer*

Two views of the immaculate Eastern Region General Manager's Wickham saloon entering Norwich station on 25 June 1975. Converted from DMBS No E50416 and DTSL No E56171, the cars carried numbers DB975005/6 and were painted into BR 'corporate blue' with raised BR logo. As well as official Departmental duties, the set was also used for a railtour on 20 July 1974, when it visited the East Suffolk line. As already mentioned, the unique unit survives, and is undergoing much needed remedial work following vandalism. The restoration is being undertaken at Butterley, to return it to working order for operation on the Llangollen Railway.

Birmingham RC&W Company three-car 'Calder Valley' Class 110

Built by:	Birmingham Railway Carriage & Wagon Company
Introduced:	June 1961
Coupling Code:	Blue Square ■
Engines in each Driving Motor:	Two Rolls-Royce six-cylinder horizontal type 180hp
Transmission:	Mechanical, Standard
Body:	57ft 6in x 9ft 3in
Weight:	DMBC 32 tons
	DMCL 31 tons 10cwt
	TSL 24 tons
Operating numbers:	DMBC 51809 to 51828, 52066 to 52075
	DMCL 51829 to 51848, 52076 to 52085
	TSL 59693 to 59712, 59808 to 59817

A total of 30 three-car 'Calder Valley' DMUs were constructed with 180hp Rolls-Royce engines, to allow for operation across the Pennines on the 'Calder Valley' route between Manchester and Leeds, via Todmorden. They were similar to the Class 104 design from the same manufacturer, but a requirement to make provision for a roof-mounted four-character headcode box resulted in changes to the front-end appearance. The Class 110s had a slanting top to the driver's windows, with a much smaller centre window, allowing for inclusion of a route indicator blind, giving them an appearance more akin to the Park Royal '103s' than the '104s'. A total of 30 units were constructed at the Smethwick works of BRC&W in two batches, and all were allocated to North Eastern Region by January 1962. The fleet was included in the BR DMU refurbishment programme, and apart from early withdrawals resulting from accident or fire damage, the last powered vehicles were not withdrawn from traffic until 1992. Most of the centre trailers, however, lasted only until 1983, the motor vehicles being formed as 'power twins'. Prior to being grouped together as Class 110, the vehicles were classified as:

110/1	Driving Motor Composite with lavatory
110/2	Driving Motor Brake Composite
163	Trailer Second with lavatory

The East Lancashire and Lakeside & Haverthwaite Railways each have one 'power twin' in preservation, and a trailer currently survives on the Battlefield Line.

Formed of DMCL No E51840, TSL No E59704 and DMBC No 51820, a brand-new BRC&W 'Calder Valley' unit is posed for official photographs in September 1961. In original green livery with light grey roof and yellow lining at waist level joining up with the front-end 'speed whisker', the unit looks particularly attractive. *Ian Allan Library*

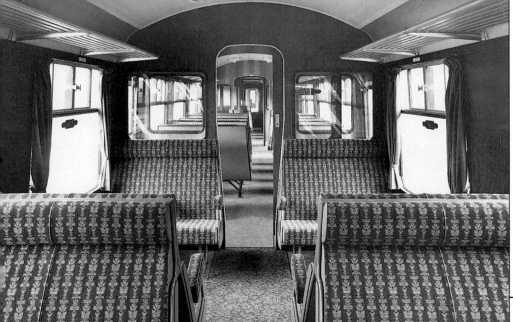

The 'Calder Valley' units were of low density design, and provided seating for 159 passengers in second class, and 24 in two first class sections. The motor brakes seated 33 'seconds' and 12 'firsts' for smokers, the motor composites 54 and 12 for non-smokers, respectively. The trailer vehicles had 72 in second class only. The first class saloons as illustrated here, were all later downgraded for standard class use.
Ian Allan Library

On one of the now-lifted centre roads in York station, on a trial run from the south on 20 June 1961, an ex-works 'Calder Valley' DMU has DMBC No E51810 nearest to the camera, and is completed with TSL No E59694 and DMCL No E51830. This was the second unit to appear from BRC&W's Smethwick Works, and this was likely to have been its first outing. *Stanley Creer*

Displaying headcode '1M42' and a destination blind showing 'Hull', DMBC No E51822 leads a three-car 'Calder Valley' unit, forming a mainline Bradford Exchange-Hull service. It is passing Crofton, southeast of Wakefield, *circa* April 1962. The roof colour is now a more serviceable dark grey. *Eric Treacy*

Operating a return excursion from Scarborough to Bradford Exchange, three BRC&W 'Calder Valley' DMUs combine to form a nine-car rake, passing near Kirkham on 21 September 1963. The roof section above the driving cab on the leading unit remains in off-white, although the remainder of the roof panels are dark grey. *Gavin Morrison*

With the roof-mounted headcode panel now out of use, BRCW Class 110/2 DMBC heads the 14.54 train from Leeds into its Skipton destination on 24 September 1976. The unit is now painted into BR 'corporate blue' livery with an all-yellow front-end. The yellow band above the leading windows shows that first class accommodation is still available at this date. The grab rails fitted immediately below the two outer cab windows were initially an additional feature, seen only on the second batch of these units, although in many cases, they were later removed.

Departing from Clayton West terminus and passing the signal cabin, the 13.00 service for Huddersfield on 5 September 1980 is formed of a BRC&W Class 110 unit, which is made up of DMBC No M52072, TSL No M59711 and DMCL No M52083. The headcode panel is now plated over. The Clayton West branch was opened in 1879 by the Lancashire & Yorkshire Railway, following authorisation given to the Huddersfield & Sheffield Junction Railway 13 years previously. At this date (1980) it was the last surviving example of a L&YR branch line. It closed to traffic in January 1983.

On 5 September 1980, the 16.15 train from Huddersfield to Wakefield Westgate passes the site of Horbury Junction station. BRC&W Class 110/1 DMCL No M51835 leads a BRC&W Class 163 TSL, but the usual Class 110/2 driving brake is missing from the formation, and has been substituted by a driving brake from a Class 101 Metro-Cammell unit.

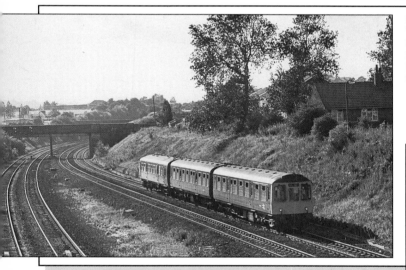

Showing the short-lived off-white/blue livery initially given to the first units of the DMU refurbishment programme, Class 163 TSL No E59811 also illustrates the distinctive end windows fitted next to the corridor connection on these vehicles, which are similar to the Class 104s from the same stable. The vehicle is receiving a classified repair inside Doncaster Works on 21 August 1981. *Colin J. Marsden*

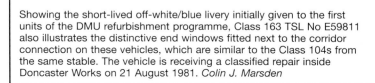

Now in blue/grey livery, a three-car Class 110 unit, with DMCL No M52076 leading, heads a five-car hybrid DMU away from Southport on 17 September 1981, forming the 13.40 service for Leeds. Waiting for a clear path from the loop alongside, Class 40 No 40182 has charge of the then daily freight working from Southport to Wigan Springs Branch.

Rare for East Anglia, a BRC&W Class 110 power twin stands in for the usual Class 150 'Sprinter' and works the 15.40 'express' from Birmingham New Street to Cambridge on 1 July 1987. DMBS No E51828 leads, and the location is between Black Bank and Pymoor. *John C. Baker*

With South Yorkshire PTE's 'MetroTrain' branding, a BRC&W Class 110 'power twin' idles in Sheffield station in rapidly diminishing light on 21 February 1985 awaiting departure as the 17.02 train for Huddersfield. Driving motor brake No E51809 is attached to driving motor No E51834. The first class compartments in both vehicles have been downgraded, and without a trailer car, the unit now has seating for 111 passengers in standard class only.

Marsden at Marsden! Retaining a TSL, a three-car BRC&W Class 110 DMU fronts a six-car hybrid formation leaving Marsden station on 14 July 1986. The train is the 13.11 from Manchester Victoria to Leeds.
Colin J. Marsden

BRCW Class 110 DMBC cars Nos E51822 and E51812 receive attention in east London's Stratford Major Depot on 22 September 1987, with Class 86/2 No 86235, then named *Novelty*, alongside.

Restored to working order and returned to original livery, the Lakeside & Haverthwaite Railway's Class 110 DMBC No M52071 and DMCL No M52077 stand in the locomotive yard at Haverthwaite, on the ex-Furness Railway, in April 1994. *Chris Dixon*

Metro-Cammell/Rolls-Royce two- or three-car Class 111

Built by:	Metropolitan-Cammell Carriage & Wagon Company
Introduced:	April 1957
Coupling Code:	Blue Square ■
Engines in each Driving Motor:	Two Rolls-Royce six-cylinder horizontal type 180hp
Transmission:	Mechanical, Standard
Body:	57ft 0in x 9ft 3in
Weight:	DMBS 33 tons
	DMCL 33 tons
	DTCL 25 tons
	TBSL 25 tons
	TSL 24 tons 10cwt
Operating numbers:	DMBS 50134 to 50137, 50280 to 50292*, 51541 to 51550
	DMCL 50270 to 50279, 50745 to 50747*, 51551 to 51560
	DTCL 56090 to 56093
	TSL 59100 to 59109, 59569 to 59572**
	TBSL 59573 to 59578
Renumbered:	All surviving cars in both 50xxx and 56xxx series renumbered to 53xxx and 54xx respectively in 1980-1

* DMBS and DMCL cars Nos 50290 to 50292 and 50745 to 50747 transferred to Class 101 after fitting with BUT (AEC) engines.
** DTCL and TSL cars transferred to work with Class 101.

Originally consisting of 50 power cars and 24 trailers, Class 111 vehicles were at first provided with separate classifications as follows:

111/1 Driving Motor Composites with lavatory
111/2 Driving Motor Brake Seconds
147 Driving Trailer Composites with lavatory (later transferred to Class 101)
164 Trailer Seconds with lavatory (later transferred to Class 101)
165 Trailer Buffet Seconds with lavatory

Constructed for general branch line and local services in the same manner as the Class 101 units, the Metro-Cammell fleet fitted with the more powerful Rolls-Royce engines at first had an identical external appearance to the others fitted with the BUT or Leyland power units. Some were still in course of construction, however, when provision for a four-character headcode box was required, and this addition changed the front-end appearance of the later units making identification between the two classes more readily apparent. Like the '101s', these vehicles used standard transmission and BUT control systems, and this allowed Rolls-Royce-engined vehicles to work attached to the Leyland or AEC cars with the 'Blue Square' coupling code. A requirement for three-car units in the particular field of operation covered by these trains was later considered unnecessary, and the Class 165 trailer buffets were withdrawn, and both the Class 147 driving trailers and the Class 164 centre trailers were removed. Consequently, all the Rolls-Royce-engined units became 'power twins'. With the aim of reducing maintenance costs, one of the two engines and transmissions was then removed from 36 Class 111 power cars between 1982-85. These were renumbered on a random basis and reclassified from driving motor composite to driving half-motor composite, and from driving motor brake to driving half-motor brake. Three of the four remaining units were transferred to Departmental stock and No 50136 (53136), which had been experimentally uprated to 230bhp, was scrapped. Renumbering was as follows:

Driving half-motor composite

50279 to 78706	51554 to 78716
50274 to 78707	51552 to 78717
50271 to 78708	51557 to 78718
53273 to 78709	51553 to 78719
53276 to 78710	51551 to 78720
53275 to 78711	51559 to 78721
53278 to 78712	51555 to 78722
53272 to 78713	51556 to 78723
53277 to 78714	51558 to 78724

Driving half-motor brake standard

50286 to 78956	51546 to 78966
50287 to 78957	51542 to 78967
50281 to 78958	51543 to 78968
53288 to 78959	51544 to 78969
53282 to 78960	51541 to 78970
53280 to 78961	51549 to 78971
53283 to 78962	51545 to 78972
53289 to 78963	51548 to 78973
53284 to 78964	51550 to 78974

The fleet was progressively withdrawn between 1986 and 1989, as second generation DMUs were introduced, and all were cut up at either Mayer Newman of Snailwell or Vic Berry of Leicester. No power cars survive in preservation, but one trailer buffet, No 59575, is destined for the Mid-Norfolk Railway.

In brand-new condition in March 1960, a three-car Rolls-Royce-engined Metro-Cammell unit is on a trial run from Washwood Heath at Aldridge, a station closed in January 1965. One of the later batch of powercars with a roof-mounted four-character headcode panel, No E51550 faces the camera. The destination blind panel has had to be moved downwards, which has resulted in the centre cab window being foreshortened. Livery is dark green with yellow lining and 'speed whisker'. *Railway Industry Association*

Displaying headcode '2E92' for a semi-fast service from Leeds to Morecambe, a three-car Class 111 unit departs from Skipton on 13 June 1974, with DMCL No E51554 leading. The original green livery has been replaced by the rather mundane, unlined BR 'corporate blue' with all-yellow front end. *Stanley Creer*

In all-blue livery but with both route indicator blind and two-character headcode panel still operational, a three-car Class 111 set awaits departure from York on 25 November 1973, forming the 09.48 service for Doncaster and Cambridge. The respective DMBS/TSL/DMCL cars are numbered E50287/59105/50274.

Nearly three years later, on 24 September 1976, the same unit operates the 12.02 train from Morecambe to Leeds, seen departing from the scheduled stop at Skipton. Leading Class 111/2 DMBS No E50287 now displays the 'Blue Square' coupling code, but in the interim the headcode panel has become redundant and one windscreen wiper has been broken off!

One of the 20 powercars constructed with a roof-mounted four-character headcode box, Class 111/1 DMCL No E51559, arrives at Leeds City station on 30 September 1978, having commenced its journey from Manchester Victoria at 07.24. Modern electronic signalling made visual observation of train reporting numbers by signalmen unnecessary, and the redundant headcode box has been plated over.

Class 111/1 DMCL No E50276 leads four Metro-Cammell cars making a stock movement to change platforms at Scarborough. There is no longer any headcode panel apparent, and the train carries the off-white/blue livery first chosen for refurbished units.

As mentioned on an earlier page, the mainly off-white livery at first given to DMUs dealt with in the refurbishment programme was soon discovered not to be serviceable, and later repaints used what was then known as 'Inter-City' livery of blue and grey. On 31 January 1981, a refurbished three-car Metro-Cammell/Rolls-Royce Class 111 unit approaches Doncaster as empty coaching stock to form a service for York. DMCL No E50279 leads TSL No E59108 and DMBS No E50286.

Restarting from the then new station of Crossflatts, a Class 111 power twin forms the 11.12 Bradford Forster Square-Keighley train on 5 February 1983. The leading vehicle is No E50272, now a driving motor standard, as the original first class seating available when it was built as a composite vehicle has been downgraded. The line above the cab windows is the orange 'safety limit' reminder for staff working beneath overhead electrified wires. An amateurish attempt appears to have been made to reintroduce 'speed whiskers' by scratching some onto the yellow paintwork.

Awaiting departure time in Ilkley station on 12 February 1983, a Class 111 power twin forms the 11.33 train for Bradford Forster Square, a service now electrified. In this case the driving motor No E50275 still shows a yellow band above the first two side windows at cantrail level, to indicate that first class seating is available. Both the DMCL and the DMBS No E50280 attached carry 'MetroTrain' branding.

Following a heavy snowstorm on 8 February 1983, a Metro Cammell/Rolls-Royce Class 111 power twin rattles along near Long Preston, seemingly undeterred by the conditions. The low position of the destination blind and the smaller centre cab window betray the fact that DMBS No E51541 was once fitted with a roof-mounted four-character headcode box. The DMSL No E51551, attached to form the 09.19 Morecambe-Leeds train, no longer has first class accommodation.

Renumbered from E50286 in August 1982, driving half-motor brake No E78956 is the rear unit of a Class 111 power twin, awaiting departure from Leeds on 4 February 1983, as the 22.43 train to Ilkley.

With the guard passing the time until departure for Leeds by filling out his log, DHBS No E78958 leads a Metro-Cammell Class 111 power twin at Skipton on 16 July 1983. *David Wilcock*

With roof-mounted headcode box removed, but retaining the small cab centre window and lowered route indicator panel, withdrawn Class 111 DHBS No E78973 is in Stratford Major Depot on 27 February 1987. Component retrieval of bogies and other underframe equipment is under way, prior to the vehicle being transported to Mayer Newman of Snailwell, where it was cut up in the following June. Components removed were later fitted to DHBS No E78960, allowing it to survive in traffic until October 1989.

Cravens/Rolls-Royce two-car Class 112 and 113

Built by:	Cravens Railway Carriage & Wagon Company (later Cravens Ltd)
Introduced:	August 1959
Coupling Code:	Blue Square ■
Engines in each Driving Motor:	One Rolls-Royce eight-cylinder horizontal type 238hp
Transmission:	Nos 51681 to 51730 Mechanical, Standard
	Nos 51731 to 51780 Hydraulic, torque converter
Body:	57ft 6in x 9ft 2in
Weight:	DMBS 29 tons 10cwt
	DMC 29 tons
Operating numbers:	DMBS 51681 to 51705, 51731 to 51755
	DMCL 51706 to 51730, 51756 to 51780

The front end of a Cravens/Rolls-Royce hydraulic DMCL No M51753. The 'Blue Square' coupling code, original 'speed whiskers' and the air horns beneath the body are all apparent in this view. *Ian Allan Library*

The 50 Rolls-Royce-engined two-car Cravens units were extremely troublesome in service, in particular those fitted with torque converter transmission that were prone to catch fire. This tendency was a result of the converter fluid overheating and feeding back into the main fuel tank. To some extent, these units were victims of circumstance, as they were constructed to operate a number of country area lines that were closed before they could be introduced upon them. As a result, the units were given duties totally unsuited to their intended role, particularly the St Pancras/Moorgate-Bedford 'Bedpan' suburban diagrams. The operating speed on these duties meant that the transmission was working almost entirely on converter drive, direct drive not being engaged until 46mph, thus the considerable overheating. These and other problems, coupled with non-standard power equipment, resulted in the type being withdrawn very early, the final examples being removed from traffic in November 1969. The fleet was allocated with the following class numbers, but withdrawal from traffic came about shortly afterwards, and use (or even knowledge) of these identities, appears minimal:

DMCL Mechanical	Class 112/1	51706 to 51730
DMBS Mechanical	Class 112/2	51681 to 51705
DMCL Hydraulic	Class 113/1	51756 to 51780
DMBS Hydraulic	Class 113/2	51731 to 51755

None of the Cravens/Rolls-Royce DMUs survive in preservation, but other similar units with AEC engines were spared from the scrap lines, and these are detailed under Class 105.

Designed with two large front-end windows with polished metal surrounds, visibility for both driver and passengers in Cravens-bodied units was very good. Having a large indicator box for combined four-figure route identification and destination blind, DMBS No M51755 leads a two-car Cravens/Rolls-Royce hydraulic DMU at Carlisle on 29 August 1966. The unit is in lined green livery with a half-yellow front warning panel, and became Class 113. *Michael Mensing*

The Cravens units were the subject of the first experimental application of a half-yellow warning panel, subsequently adopted on BR for use with the green livery. Prior to this, in 1961, one of the original 'speed whiskered' type forms a local service from Ipswich to Cambridge, near Thurston. This is a unit with mechanical standard transmission, which became Class 112. The type does not have the roof-mounted four-figure headcode box incorporating a destination panel. Instead, a two-figure box is built in below the driving cab windows, and the destination panel, although in the same position, is a separate fixture.
John C. Baker

Augmented with a BR Derby Works Class 127 trailer No M59623, a Cravens/Rolls-Royce two-car hydraulic DMU arrives at Kentish Town station on 2 March 1963, forming the 13.10 service from Barking. DMCL No M51761 leads, with DMBS No M51732 on the rear. The 'Blue Square' coupling code given to these units is clearly visible on each side of the front yellow warning panel.
John N. Faulkner

Operating the last day of passenger services to Bacup on 3 December 1966, a train for Manchester Victoria is formed of a Rolls-Royce-powered Cravens unit with DMCL No M51690 leading. One of the 25 two-car units fitted with standard mechanical transmission, these were not so troubled with overheating and consequent fires as their hydraulic counterparts. However, they were still to suffer the fate of a very early withdrawal, primarily resulting from having non-standard power equipment.
Gavin Morrison

With DMCL mechanical No M51711 leading, two Cravens/Rolls-Royce twins make up a four-car train waiting to depart from Blackburn on 1 September 1962 as the 10.47 service from Colne to Blackpool Central. Each driving composite vehicle provided 12 first class and 51 second class seats, with the motor brakes having 52 second class seats only.
Michael Mensing

With the line to Bury curving away to the left, the 13.20 through train from Manchester Victoria to Colne approaches Bolton on 18 March 1966, formed of a Cravens/Rolls-Royce two-car hydraulic unit, motor composite No M51756 leading. Together with No M51780, this car was the last to be introduced from the Sheffield works of Cravens, in July 1960. It was withdrawn in April 1969, seven years after No M51780, which was cut up at Derby works in September 1962, following serious fire damage. *R. J. Farrell*

On 20 April 1968, a Class 112 Cravens/Rolls-Royce mechanical power twin enters Leyton Midland Road station, working a Barking-Kentish Town train. Surviving just long enough to receive BR 'corporate blue' livery with all-yellow front end, DMCL No M51712 and DMBS No M51687 were both withdrawn from service seven months later. *John N. Faulkner*

Only three of the 100 Class 112/113 cars were scrapped at the premises of G. Cohen, near Kettering, DMCL vehicles Nos 51712, 51714 and 51725. One of these is pictured at the scrapyard on 30 March 1978, 10 years after being withdrawn, but still two years before eventually being cut up. *Kevin Lane*

BR Derby two-car Class 114

Built by:	British Rail Derby Works	
Introduced:	October 1956	
Coupling Code:	Blue Square ■	
Engines in each Driving Motor:	Two BUT (Leyland) six-cylinder horizontal type 230hp*	
Transmission:	Mechanical, Standard**	
Body:	64ft 6in x 9ft 3in	
Weight:	DMBS	35 tons 10cwt
	DTCL	29 tons or 31 tons
Operating numbers:	DMBS	50000 to 50049
	DTCL	56001 to 56049
Renumbered:	All surviving cars in both 50xxx and 56xxx series renumbered to 53xxx and 54xxx respectively in 1980-1	

54034 to 55933	Ø to 54900
54016 to 54901	
54036 to 55932	Ø to 54902
54009 to 54903	
54015 to 54904	
53018 to 55928	
53015 to 55929	
53010 to 55930	
53040 to 55931	
53032 to 55932	

Ø 55xxx series number first given in error

* Powercar No E50000 temporarily fitted with two experimental eight-cylinder Rolls-Royce 238hp engines and hydraulic twin disc torque converter.

** Powercar No E50049 temporarily fitted with Self-Changing Gears Ltd automatic four-speed box.

Although these units were given TOPS classification 114 (initially the driving trailers were Class 148), the 50 two-car DMU twins under this heading were the first vehicles introduced under the Modernisation Plan proper, and the first to be given 5xxxx numbers instead of the 7xxxx series used previously. Designed for Eastern Region local and branch line services around the Lincoln area, the units were justly described as 'Derby Heavyweights'. Aluminium construction had proved to be expensive, as well as troublesome, and Derby works now opted for steel bodies on the longer underframe, making the units more robust by far than the 'Derby Lightweights'. They were also the first of many types to have the three-window, raked back front end which was to become a Derby hallmark.

The '114' fleet was accepted as part of BR's 1970s DMU refurbishment programme, and apart from withdrawals resulting from accident damage, the units remained in service for over 30 years, being taken out of traffic between 1988 and 1992. In 1987-9, five driving motors and five driving trailers were converted for use as Parcels Sector cars and renumbered as detailed above. Their life was brief, however, and all were withdrawn in November 1990. Nos 55929 and 54904 (ex-53015 and 54015) became Advanced Passenger Train test, development and training coaches Nos ADB97775/6 at RTC Derby. These were later taken on by Central Services, then by EWS/Transrail as a route learning and inspection saloon. Driving motor No 53019 (ex-50019) and driving trailer No 56006 (ex-54006) are in preservation at the Midland Railway Centre, and driving trailer No 54047 (56047) is at the Strathspey Railway.

With the obligatory tail lamp, a 'Derby Heavyweight' twin arrives at Sheffield Victoria in the late 1950s. Displaying its 'Blue Square' coupling code, driving motor No E50016 is still in original condition. *Les Nixon*

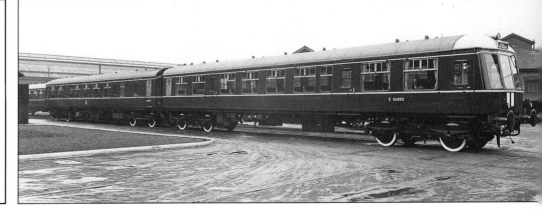

Numerically the first Modernisation Plan production DMU is rolled out for official photographs at Derby Carriage Works in October 1956. DTCL No E56000 is nearest to the camera, with DMBS No E50000 behind. Features are a white fibreglass cab roof canopy, with a roof marker light above the destination blind, and two-figure route indicator panel below the centre windscreen. The livery is green with cream lining-out, the green being darker than malachite. Curtains are provided for the first class windows only. *Ian Allan Library*

Two 'Derby Heavyweight' twins form a service for Sheffield Victoria on 19 July 1960. Departing from Retford and joining the Sheffield line at Whisker Hill Junction, the leading driving motor brake now displays 'speed whiskers', and the white cab roof canopy has been painted to match the dark grey of the other roof panels. *Stanley Creer*

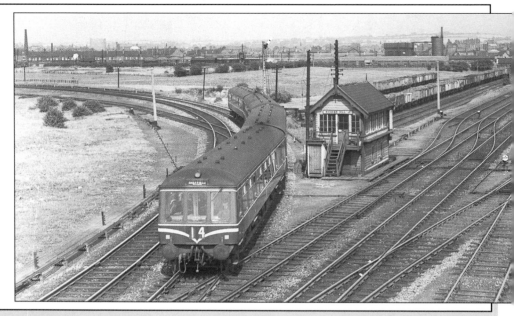

Beneath the attractive but decaying overall roof at Firsby station on 9 July 1969, DMBS No E50001 leads, and awaits departure for Skegness. Now attached to one of the eight 31-ton driving trailers, No E56007, the original lined green paintwork and 'speed whiskers' have been displaced by BR 'corporate blue' and a half-yellow front-end warning panel. Firsby station closed to passenger traffic in October 1970, and the site is now a grass-covered field, betraying no evidence of its former railway connection.
John A. M. Vaughan

When out-shopped after painting, overall BR blue livery with full-yellow front end could, at first, appear quite attractive. When work-stained, however, it looked very drab. Class 114 DMBS No E50003 and Class 148 DTCL No 56014 stand at Grantham on 25 September 1976, forming the 14.06 train for Nottingham.

The 18.00 service for Cleethorpes prepares to move away from New Holland Pier on 24 May 1980, formed of two Class 114 'Derby Heavyweight' twins. The station is in a state of disrepair, as it was scheduled to close once construction of the Humber Bridge was completed. With the route indicator panel plated over and marker lights inserted, driving motor No E50044 leads cars E56029, E56013 and E50026.

Stabled at Sheffield on the night of 28 January 1980, DMBS No E50007 leads DTCL No E56017. Following refurbishment, both vehicles have been painted into the short-lived off-white livery with blue stripe. The route indicator panel has been removed and front lights fitted. The original top marker light is still in situ, but is now out of use.
Colin J. Marsden

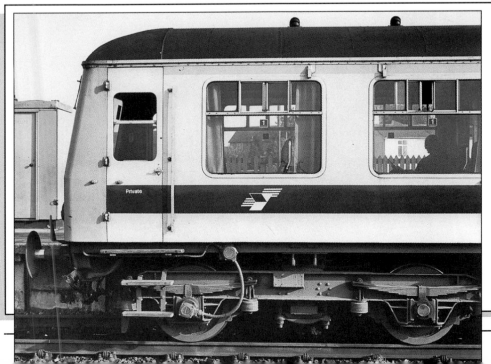

The front end of Class 148 driving trailer No E56023 at Barton-on-Humber on 24 May 1980. The logo denotes sponsorship by the South Yorkshire Passenger Transport Authority.

Livery transition. The 11.38 Doncaster-Cleethorpes train commences its journey on 31 January 1981, formed of a Class 114 'Derby Heavyweight' twin. In white/blue colours, DMBS No E50018 leads DTCL No E56001, which is in blue and grey 'InterCity' livery. Similar in appearance to the BR Derby Classes 107 and 108 units, but built on long frames, the '114s' have four windows between the passenger doors, instead of the three on the other types.

Smartly turned out in blue/grey livery, a Class 114 twin operates the 12.05 service from Newark Northgate to Cleethorpes on 1 September 1980, and passes Melton Ross, near Barnetby. Both the route indicator panel and the top marker light have been removed from driving trailer No E56040, which leads driving motor brake No E50014. The trailers have 62 seats in second class and 12 in first class. The motor brake provides seating for 62 in second class only.

A Class 114 twin brings up the rear of a mixed formation of DMU stock on 2 September 1980. Class 148 DTCL No E56036 is nearest to the camera, as the 08.45 Hull-Scarborough service negotiates the level crossing on departure from Filey.

With one of the two new marker lights in operation, Class 114 driving motor No E50020 and driving trailer No E56021 await departure from Leeds, on the very wet night of 4 February 1983. The train is the 22.35 for Skipton.

Now reclassified from '148' to '114', trailer composite No E56044 idles at Bradford Forster Square station on 12 February 1983 prior to departure for Keighley at 14.12. In the adjacent platform, a Metro-Cammell Class 111 DMC No E51555, with a working destination blind, heads the 13.55 for Ilkley.

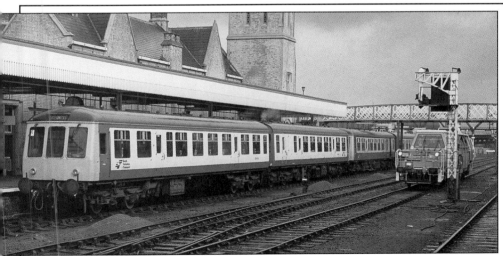

At Lincoln on 26 August 1986, Class 114 DTSL No 54004 and DMBS No 53045 are formed with '114s' Nos 53005 and 54022 to work the 16.16 train from Lincoln to Skegness. The leading vehicle has been downgraded from a composite with first class to a driving trailer standard with 74 standard class seats, and the leading unit has been painted into an experimental brown and cream livery for the South Yorkshire PTA. *Mick Alderman*

A close-up of the branding on the leading vehicle.

Associated with Lincoln depot and the Lincoln area for nearly all of their existence, Class 114 units were still on hand inside the depot when it closed down in 1987. With Cravens Class 105 Departmental vehicle No TDB977125 alongside, driving brake No E53047 displays 'Lincoln' in the destination blind. The vehicle was originally numbered 50047.

Branded 'Express Parcels' and carrying the 'Red Star' logo, driving motor brake No E53027 is at York on 2 September 1987, as part of a Parcels Sector train for Cambridge. This vehicle was one of the six adapted for use with parcels traffic which were later painted with a red stripe on a blue or blue/grey livery. Driving trailer No 54041 (previously No 56041) is attached but not in view. Both vehicles were short-lived in this guise and were withdrawn before the end of 1990.

Classified as a driving trailer parcels and mail van (DTPMV), ex-DTCL No 54034 stands outside Ilford Works on 5 June 1987, after conversion from a passenger vehicle. Unfortunately the new number 55933 on the bodyside was later realised to be incorrect, as the 55xxx series applied only to motorised vehicles. A similar error occurred with No 55932, which was renumbered from 54036. Both numbers were later changed to 54900 and 54902, respectively. In all, five Class 114 twins were gutted and rebuilt for Parcels Sector use.

The new interior of Class 114 DTPMV No 55933 (later No 54900) after conversion at Ilford 'B' Shop in June 1987. Roller shutter doors have been fitted and the immediate floor area has been strengthened to allow for loaded 'Brutes' to be wheeled in.

Approaching Potters Bar on 22 December 1987, a southbound Class 114 'Express Parcels' unit is formed of DMBPV vehicles Nos 55930 leading 55931. Previously numbered 53010 and 53040, respectively, the train is in original Parcels Sector blue livery with a broad red band at waist height, bordered with a white stripe. 'Express Parcels' is displayed in what used to be the destination panel.

With the Leeds Hilton hotel as a backdrop, Royal Mail-liveried DMUs pass through Leeds on 15 March 1988. With its roller shutter doors now painted with red and yellow stripes, the leading driving trailer is the second of the Class 114 type to have been wrongly numbered after conversion for Parcels Sector use; the figures 55932 on the bodyside were later changed to 54902. Behind the leading unit is a pair of Gloucester RC&W Class 128 parcels units, both in the same livery. *David Wilcock*

When this photograph was taken at Arley, on the Severn Valley Railway, it was rare for any BR locomotives or stock to operate over a private line. On 14 October 1989, however, Class 114 set No TO22 visited the line as part of a diesel gala, and is operating the 10.40 Bridgnorth-Bewdley shuttle service. With Regional number prefixes now omitted, driving trailer No 54047 leads driving motor brake No 53002. *Colin J. Marsden*

Class 114 set No TO21 of Tyseley, formed of DTSL No 54012 and DMBS No 53021, form the 10.18 Lichfield Trent Valley-Redditch Cross-City service on 29 August 1990, and enter Birmingham New Street station. At this time, these vehicles were the oldest DMUs still in operation on BR passenger services.

No longer required for use as parcels cars, Class 114 vehicles Nos 54904 and 55929 were taken on by Central Services and painted into its livery of grey, red and yellow. Later, the unit was transferred to EWS/Transrail and used as a route-learning DMU based at Bescot. On 24 June 1996, it passes through Harlech station, heading for Pwllheli. Both cars are carrying their fourth allocated number, the driving motor No 977775 having previously been 50015, 53015 and 55929, and the driving trailer No 977776 having carried numbers 56015, 54015 and 54904. *John Stretton*

BR Derby four-car Class 115

Built by:	British Rail Derby Works
Introduced:	March 1960
Coupling Code:	Blue Square ■
Engines in each Driving Motor:	Two BUT (Leyland Albion) six-cylinder horizontal type 230hp
Transmission:	Mechanical, Standard
Body:	64ft 0in x 9ft 3in

Weight:	DMBS	38 tons
	TS	28 tons
	TCL	30 tons

Operating numbers:	DMBS	51651 to 51680, 51849 to 51900
	TS	59649 to 59663, 59713 to 59718, 59725 to 59744
	TCL	59664 to 59678, 59719 to 59724, 59745 to 59764

Designed for the outer suburban services from Marylebone, Derby Works produced 82 four-car high-density units between March and December 1960. Other than a few vehicles withdrawn early because of accident damage, the fleet was included in the 1970s refurbishment programme, and remained in service until the Chiltern Lines upgrading, followed by the progressive introduction of new Class 165/0 'Chiltern Turbo' units in 1990-2. The general layout of the trains resembled their Class 127 counterparts on the St Pancras suburban services, with the same lack of gangways and the two toilets both contained only in the trailer composite vehicle. The interior design, however, was much improved over the '127s', and removed the bus-type atmosphere characteristic of most of the DMU fleets up to that time. The powercars were the first to be fitted with the 230hp Leyland Albion engine. Prior to the complete four-car train being classified 115, the vehicles were initially given the following TOPS identities:

115	Driving Motor Brake Second
173	Trailer Second
177	Trailer Composite with lavatory

A total of 13 driving motor brakes are the subject of preservation, together with five trailer standard and two trailer composite cars. Lines currently having examples of the type are the Buckinghamshire Railway Centre, the Lavender Line, the Midland Railway Centre, the West Somerset, Mid-Norfolk, South Devon and Strathspey Railways. In addition, the National Railway Museum is involved with motor brake No M51562.

High-backed seating, individual lights beneath the luggage racks, carpeting and wood veneer are all features of the first class accommodation in the BR Derby Marylebone trailer composite vehicle. Occupants had one of the two toilet compartments to themselves, with the other separating the first and second class saloons. *British Rail*

Externally, the Marylebone suburban units were virtually identical to the Class 127 'Bedpan' trains on the St Pancras-Bedford services. New from Derby Works in July 1960, a four-car set is posed for an official photograph. The livery is a dark olive green with cream lining and 'speed whiskers'. A route indicator panel is above the destination blind in the centre window, and two marker lights are fitted. The white roof panels were soon painted dark grey, and the square buffers were also short-lived. The vehicles are DMBS No M51864, TS No M59726, TCL No M59746 and DMBS No M51863. *British Rail*

Two four-car Marylebone suburban sets form a High Wycombe to Marylebone local service in June 1962, passing West Ruislip. Driving motor brake No M51671, leading, has a half-yellow front-end warning panel in place of the original 'speed whiskers' and retains square buffers. Above the 'Blue Square' coupling codes on either side of the panel have been placed overhead electrification warning stickers. *C. R. Lewis Coles*

Led by DMBS No M51668 with oval buffers, a four-car BR Derby Marylebone line unit departs from Brackley Central on 16 October 1965, forming the Monday to Friday, once-a-day semi-fast service from Nottingham Victoria for the London terminus. The train was scheduled to depart from Marylebone at 08.38 and returned from Nottingham at 12.20. Brackley Central station closed with the remainder of the Great Central main line north of Aylesbury on 5 September 1966. *Rodney Lissenden*

Leaving Aylesbury on 15 February 1976, BR Derby Class 115 DMBS No M51674 leads the 14.12 Sunday service for Amersham. The unit is now in overall unlined BR 'corporate blue' livery, with a full-yellow front end. Standard round buffer heads are now fitted to the Class 115 fleet.

A typical Marylebone scene of the 1970s, with the 13.10 departure for Aylesbury idling at the platform and adding to the 'atmosphere'. Leading is the last DMBS to be built, No M51900. It retains a destination blind, but the roof-mounted route indicator panel has been blanked off.

Four Class 115 units are visible on depot at Marylebone on 9 March 1978, DMBS No M51876 being at the service platform on the right. Following introduction of the 'Chiltern Turbo' units, which are maintained at the new Aylesbury depot, Marylebone depot was closed and has since been demolished.

The short-lived off-white livery with blue band at first given to refurbished units did not appear on many Class 115 vehicles. The majority were scheduled for attention quite late on in the scheme of things, and before they entered works for attention it was realised that the prime colour was unserviceable. Attached to three vehicles, in what was initially termed 'Inter-City' livery, DMBS No M51664 heads the 15.10 train for Aylesbury at Marylebone station on 18 July 1983.

In blue/grey livery, a Class 115 unit approaches Marylebone station on 5 July 1984, and passes two others of the same type in the service platform next to the maintenance depot. The driving motor brake vehicles seated 78 in second class. The all-second class trailers had provision for 106 seats, and the trailer composite vehicles had 30 first class and 40 in second. *John Glover*

BR Derby Class 115 units in echelon on the approaches to Marylebone station on 26 January 1985. All standard four-car units, the left-hand one is at the fuelling point, the centre train is heading for Aylesbury, and the right-hand set is an arrival from the same town. *David Wilcock*

Passengers aboard the 19.25 train for Banbury, steam up the inside of the windows of Class 115 DMBS No M51674, which will shortly head away from Marylebone on the cold evening of 7 February 1985. Driving motor brakes were fitted with power sanders for rail adhesion during 1981. In this view, the device can be seen between the bogie.

Complete with its then newly-applied 'Chiltern Line' branding, DMBS No M51676 stands at the Marylebone buffer-stops on 10 June 1986.

In the winter snows of 1986, a four-car Class 115 unit approaches Gerrards Cross with a stopping train from Banbury. In the distance another unit of the same type is in the platform loop with a 'Chiltern Line' service that is heading in the opposite direction. *David Wilcock*

Class 115 DMBS No M51899 was the first British Rail DMU vehicle to be officially named, and to carry cast metal nameplates. Christened at Aylesbury as part of an Open Day there on 20 June 1987, the plates 'Aylesbury College SILVER JUBILEE 1987' remained in situ until the car was withdrawn in August 1992, after which one was presented to the college. No 51889 has been preserved and can be seen at the Buckinghamshire Railway Centre.

During the latter part of the 1980s, some Class 115 vehicles were transferred to Tyseley depot to assist with operating Birmingham Cross-City services, as a number of the ageing DMUs in the area had been withdrawn from traffic. As a result, some Class 108 driving trailers and trailer standard cars were brought in to augment the '115s' at peak times. At West Ruislip on 30 June 1987, a '108' driving trailer and a trailer second make up half of the consist of the four-car unit forming the 17.55 Marylebone-High Wycombe service (showing 'Blackpool' in the destination blind!). On the left, the two-car unit consists of Class 115 DMBS No M51679 and Class 108 DT No 54257. After leaving the siding and entering the station, this hybrid twin will form the 18.48 train from West Ruislip to Marylebone.

With a Network SouthEast logo below the centre cab window, Class 115 DMBS No M51676 stands inside Marylebone depot on 22 July 1988. A new illuminated 'white on blue' blind has been fitted in place of the older type. Also, a more sympathetic 'Sorry' has been added to the previously terse 'Not in Service'.

During the period of livery transition, Class 115 TCs Nos 59755 and 59732 receive attention in Marylebone depot on the same day. Painted into new Network SouthEast (NSE) livery, the vehicles stand between two driving motors that are still in blue and grey. The Regional prefix 'M' is omitted on repainting.

Allocated to Tyseley depot, an eight-car DMU hybrid, formed of sets T403 and T307, forms the 09.11 'express' from Burton upon Trent to Skegness on 31 August 1987. The train is passing Hubbert's Bridge, west of Boston, and the leading unit No T403 is formed of Class 115 DMBS No M51852, which is leading two Class 127 Trailers, Nos M59616 and 59641, with Class 116 DMS No M53106 at the rear. *John C. Baker*

A busy scene at Stourbridge Junction on 28 November 1987. With the West Midlands Passenger Transport Executive logo painted in white on the yellow front end, Tyseley Class 115 unit No T401, led by DMBS No M51662, departs as the 10.32 Birmingham New Street-Great Malvern train. In the opposite platform, Class 114 unit No T223 also sports the PTE logo and waits to depart in the opposite direction as the 11.00 service for Birmingham New Street. On the left, Class 121 single-car unit No T133 arrives as the 10.47 from Stourbridge Town.

Successfully attempting to impersonate a Class 121 or 122 single-car unit, Class 115 Driving Motor Brake No M51884 passes Barrow Hill (Staveley) on 29 March 1990. The vehicle has been overhauled at the BRML works at Doncaster and is going back to Tyseley depot. Normally, a move of this nature would involve a two, three or four-car unit. *David Wilcock*

The Tyseley Depot 'chained bear' logo on the front of Class 115 DMBS No 51862 of Tyseley set No T410.

On 28 March 1987, the 'Mickleover Hypothesis' railtour passes the old station buildings at Egginton Junction, as it travels along the BR test track to Mickleover. Both units are of Class 115, with the NSE-liveried one consisting of vehicles Nos 51889, 59763, 59727 and 51659. The blue and grey set is made up of Nos M51666, 59750, 59739 and 51667. *John Tuffs*

The 10.15 Marylebone-Banbury train emerges from St John's Wood tunnel on 24 July 1988, and crosses the West Coast main line. Only the TSL has so far received NSE livery, the other three cars of the Class 115 unit being still in blue/grey. DMBS No M51883 leads.

As the days of the Marylebone suburban '115s' came to an end, availability resulted in both two and three-car formations operating on 'Chiltern Lines' services, as well as the normal four-car units. On 19 March 1992, a Class 115 'power twin' approaches the London terminus to augment the standard four-car 15.10 Marylebone-Aylesbury train. Both DMBS vehicles, Nos 51887 and 51659, are in the red, white, blue and grey colours of Network SouthEast.

On 29 July 1992, the 19.11 departure from Marylebone for Aylesbury was the last 'Chiltern Lines' train to use Class 115 DMUs, all services having been taken over by Class 165/0 'Chiltern Turbos'. With an appropriate headboard, a very well-patronised eight-car '115' combination departs from the London terminus, consisting of a three-car set (Nos 51677, 59761 and 51875), a four-car unit (Nos 51886, 59678, 59728 and 51872) and a single DMBS No 51659 bringing up the rear.

Two DMBS Class 115 cars, Nos 51677 and 51655, stand at Isfield station, on the Lavender Line, on 24 April 1993, after purchase for preservation.

BR Derby three-car Class 116/130

Built by:	British Rail Derby Works	
Introduced:	April 1957	
Coupling Code:	Blue Square ■	
Engines in each Driving Motor:	Two BUT (Leyland) six-cylinder horizontal type 150hp	
Transmission:	Mechanical, Standard	
Body:	64ft 0in x 9ft 3in	
Weight:	DMBS	38 tons 10cwt
	DMS	35 tons 10cwt
	TC	28 tons 10cwt
	TS	28 tons 10cwt
Operating numbers:	DMBS	50050 to 50091, 50818 to 50870, 51128 to 51140
	DMS	50092 to 50133, 50871 to 50923, 51141 to 51153
	TC	59000 to 59031, 59326 to 59376, 59438 to 59448
	TS	59032 to 59041
Renumbered:	All surviving cars in 50xxx series renumbered to 53xxx in 1980-1.	

Designed specifically for suburban duties, the three-car high density units that became Class 116, were not really much of an improvement on some steam-hauled stock that they replaced. Seating was cramped, with the door to each bay having droplight windows, providing occupants with minimum comfort and maximum draughts. There were no toilet facilities, and no gangways between the vehicles in each three-car set. This effectively isolated passengers within each vehicle, and denied through access to staff in case of an emergency. For the short trips for which they were presumably intended, these conditions were tolerable. For longer journeys, however, the trains offered little improvement over competing bus services, and on occasions, when grossly overloaded, it was not unknown for a vehicle body to sag under the weight, preventing passenger doors from being opened. The fleet totalled 216 powercars and 104 trailers, and all were initially allocated to Western Region at Tyseley and Cardiff, for use in the Birmingham area and in South Wales. Later six powercars were converted for parcels traffic and were given class number 130. Two were withdrawn after fire damage in 1972, and the remaining four went under the torch in 1987-8, having been reinstated for passenger service. Meanwhile in 1985, four further driving cars were transferred for parcels traffic and had seats removed. Two of the vehicles, Nos 53051 and 53072, allocated to Chester depot, were both withdrawn a few years later, in 1988. Due to a severe stock shortage, the remaining two vehicles, Nos 53083 and

53820, had seating reinstated and were put to work on Barking-Gospel Oak services as the powercars for unit No L307. Later transferred to Bristol and then Cardiff, both survived in traffic until the summer of 1992. Prior to the complete units in passenger service becoming known as Class 116, the individual vehicles were classified as:

116/1	Driving Motor Second
116/2	Driving Motor Brake Second
172	Trailer Second
175	Trailer Composite

The '116' fleet was an early inclusion in the DMU refurbishment programme that commenced in the 1970s, and as a result large numbers received the first revised livery of off-white with a blue stripe. At the same time, the opportunity was taken to partly rebuild all the vehicles remaining in service with gangway connections, and to include a lavatory compartment in the centre of some trailers, reducing seating capacity from 102 to 88. By 1988, nearly all the stock had been dealt with in this way, making the units more compatible with later high-density builds. The last vehicles were not withdrawn until the middle 1990s. A complete three-car unit has been preserved on the Swansea Vale Railway, and other vehicles have been obtained for various use by the Battlefield Line, and by the Chacewater, East Kent, Gloucestershire Warwickshire, and Paignton & Dartmouth Railways.

New from Derby works in April 1957, the first three-car suburban unit that was to become Class 116, faces the official camera. Having bodyside slam-doors with droplights to each seating bay, and lacking gangway connections or toilet facilities, the unit was generally considered a retrograde step in railcar design — and the unlined Brunswick green livery also tended to give the units a mundane appearance. Featuring four marker lights, a destination blind showing 'Birmingham Snow Hill', 'speed whiskers' and white fibreglass cab roof canopy, however, the front-end appearance at least was quite acceptable. DMBS No W50050 leads TC No W59000 and DMS No W50092. The TC vehicle was withdrawn in December 1982, but the two driving cars lasted in traffic for a further 10 years. *British Rail*

Another official photograph. This time, the leading vehicle is DMS No W51150 of the 1958 batch, fitted with a two-figure route indicator panel in place of the centre marker light, and with the roof marker light also omitted. The TC is No W59447 and the DMBS at the rear is No W51137. *British Rail*

A Tyseley-allocated three-car high-density unit of the 1957 batch enters Wednesbury station on 28 May 1960, heading for Wellington. The station closed to passengers in March 1972, but a rail service is returning to the town with the commencement of the Midland Metro tramway system. The new depot for the trams is at Wednesbury. *R. C. Riley*

With motor brake No W51138 leading, a three-car 1958-built Derby unit passes Leigh Bridge crossing, between Crowcombe Heathfield and Stogumber, on 24 August 1963. The train is the 11.52 from Taunton to Minehead. The Minehead branch closed to passengers in January 1971 and is now operated by the West Somerset Railway, which has some BR Derby Class 115 vehicles in preservation, but no '116's. *Peter W. Gray*

In October 1969, Western Region introduced an airfreight parcels service running overnight between Bristol and Hayes, from where the consignment was taken by road to Heathrow Airport. Two Class 116 driving motor vehicles and two GUV vans were adapted at Newton Abbot to form a four-car unit, DMBS No W51137 and DMS No W51150 being stripped of seating for the purpose, and becoming Class 130.

Seen outside the National Carriers Ltd premises at Reading, both driving motors were withdrawn in 1972 following a fire. Another four Class 116 powercars, Nos W50819, 50862, 50872 and 50915, were also converted for parcels duties, where they remained until the early 1980s. Seats were then restored and the vehicles recommenced passenger operation again, being finally withdrawn in 1987-8. *Colin J. Marsden collection*

If unlined green livery was thought to be an uninspired livery choice, then the new BR 'corporate blue', with a full-yellow front end, was hardly an improvement. Leading the 12.25 local train from Birmingham New Street to Leamington Spa on 14 September 1974, Class 116/2 motor brake No M50085 displays Tyseley diagram number '529' in the cab window. The yellow line at cantrail level on the second trailer composite vehicle shows the position of first class seating. The seemingly rural setting is between Warwick and Leamington Spa. The motor brake powercars seated 65 in second class (later standard class) and the driving motor second vehicles packed in 95.

Class 116/1 DMS No M50113 faces the camera as a Nuneaton-Coventry shuttle service arrives at its destination on 5 January 1975. Class 175 trailer composite No W59012 and Class 116/2 DMBS No M50051 complete the train. Showing 'Special' on the destination blind, the DMS retains its original four marker lights at this stage.

Seen from between locomotives stabled at Ranelagh Bridge fuelling yard, a Paddington to Slough parcels service begins its journey on 21 May 1975. Class 130 No W50915 hauls a motley collection of vehicles in use for parcels traffic, with classmate No W50819 propelling from the rear.

Makeshift parcels trains were not uncommon in the 1970s. On 20 March 1976, Class 130 parcels car No W50862 heads down the relief line at Southall, with a GUV (possibly ex-Railair) and a Pressed Steel Company Class 121 single-car unit on the rear, which has been commandeered for the occasion.

One man and his dog alight from Class 116 DMU set No C354 at Penarth on 13 August 1975. Displaying the correct 'C2' route code for a cross-Cardiff stopping service, the train will now return to Rhymney.

One of the first Class 116 units to have gangways fitted and a lavatory compartment installed, No P317 arrives at Newton Abbot on 2 July 1979, to form the 12.05 train to Paignton. The first revised livery for refurbished units of off-white with blue waistline band was attractive when kept clean. The leading DMBS now retains just two marker lights, and the route indicator panel has been removed.

The 15.32 Treherbert-Barry Island train arrives at Tonypandy on 14 September 1979, formed of refurbished Cardiff Canton-allocated unit No C316. The powercars, Nos W50856 and W50909, and the trailer composite No W59364 are all now gangwayed.

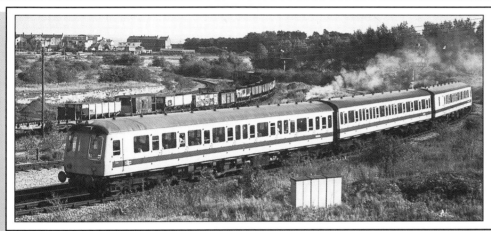

With only the left cab window given a chrome finish, Class 116 DMS No W50131 looks decidedly 'one-eyed' as it makes a smoky path into Barry on 15 September 1979, forming the 15.50 train from Barry Island to Treherbert. The unit has been gangwayed upon refurbishment, but the trailer has not been fitted with a lavatory compartment.

Operating Tyseley diagram No 543, as indicated in the cab window, the 10.42 Longbridge-Four Oaks Birmingham 'Cross-City' local service emerges from New Street South tunnel into Birmingham New Street station on 22 March 1980. The refurbished Class 116 DMS No M50895 leading retains two marker lights and the destination blind, but there is no visible trace of its original two-character route indicator box.

DMU vehicles that were not refurbished when the off-white/blue livery was in vogue, went straight from old unlined blue to the new blue/grey design, initially reserved for Inter-City stock. With the route indicator panel plated over, Class 116 DMBS No Sc50825 still awaits a full refurbishment, whereas the trailer composite and the driving motor have been upgraded and repainted. The 15.00 train from Glasgow Central to East Kilbride passes between Thorntonhall and Hairmyres on 25 January 1981.

The unusual sight of a four-car Class 116 combination leaving Barking as the 17.10 train for Gospel Oak on 8 August 1981. DMS No M50101 leads the usual TC and DMBS vehicles, with an additional powercar, No M50893, on the rear. All four vehicles await refurbishment.

The noon departure from Merthyr Tydfil to Cardiff Central rolls into the platform at Taffs Well on 10 June 1982. Class 116 set No C318 is led by DMS No W50917. The car is refurbished and gangwayed, together with the other two vehicles, TC No W59369 and DMBS No W50864.

With DMBS No E53867 (renumbered from 50867) nearest to the camera, a three-car BR Derby Class 116 and a two-car Cravens Class 105 unit, both still in all-over blue livery, form the 16.30 Wickford-Southminster train passing Burnham-on-Crouch on 12 September 1983. The unintentional reflection of the author in the cab window shows him holding a camera in the upright position, and not, as might be interpreted, attempting a highland fling!

Approaching Southminster branch terminus on the same day, DMBS No E53853, TC No E59367 and DMS No E53894 comprise the Class 116 unit forming the 15.08 local service from Wickford. Refurbished and painted in blue and grey, the train is a recent transfer to Eastern Region from Scotland.

Forming the 14.28 train from Leamington Spa to Birmingham Moor Street, a refurbished and gangwayed Class 116 unit descends Hatton bank on 29 February 1994. The logo of the West Midlands PTE, usually on the blue bodyside of the units, is painted in white on the yellow front end of DMBS No M53850. With a lavatory compartment fitted into the trailer composite, the centre vehicle is strictly now a TCL. The powercar was previously numbered M50850, but was changed to avoid the BR TOPS computer identifying it as a Class 50.

Shake, rattle and roll seems to be the order of the day for passengers, as BR Derby Class 116 DMBS No M53073 leads a particularly bizarre combination of DMU vehicles through Lower Basildon, near Goring, on 5 August 1987. The service is the 13.10 semi-fast from Reading to Birmingham New Street, and the vehicles at the rear of Tyseley set No T416 comprise Classes 115, 104 (still in plain blue) and 121.

BREL Doncaster Works on 3 October 1987. Following collision damage, the front end of a withdrawn 'Welsh Valleys' Class 116 powercar is in the process of being welded onto the body of Class 117 DMS No 51396. The remainder of the '116' vehicle was cut up at Vic Berry's at Leicester two months earlier, in August 1987. The Class 117, with its Class 116-look front end, currently continues in service on Silverlink Trains' services between Clapham Junction and Willesden Junction, and is further illustrated in the Class 117 section, on page 153.

Following the launch of Network SouthEast (NSE) on 10 June 1986, locomotives and rolling stock under the sector's jurisdiction were painted into a new red, white, blue and grey livery when a repaint was scheduled — and often before one was scheduled. With a Class 128 Parcels Car attached to the rear, Class 117 set No L402 approaches Paddington on 27 December 1986, forming the 10.54 local service from Reading. With regional number prefixes no longer applying, DMBS No 51335 leads. Also completing its journey, the 10.05 InterCity HST service from Bristol Temple Meads is led by Class 43 powercar No 43017.

Except for Reading depot, unit set number prefixes reflected the depot of origin, such as 'B' for Bristol, 'C' for Cardiff, 'P' for Plymouth, and 'T' for Tyseley. Reading used an 'L' for London Division - with just one exception. Motor Brake No W51340 leads the 12.54 Reading-Paddington train near Langley on 22 April 1987, clearly displaying set No R405.

During the period when NSE motive power and coaching stock was being re-liveried into sector colours, it was not uncommon to see both old and new paintwork together. One such instance occurred before the camera at Lower Basildon, near Goring, on 5 August 1987. Class 117 DMU No L411 in red, white, blue and grey, forms the 13.33 service from Oxford to Reading, while '117' set No L419 passes, travelling in the opposite direction, as the 14. 10 train from Reading to Oxford.

A new station on Network SouthEast 'Chiltern Lines' was opened at Haddenham & Thame Parkway on 3 October 1987, and a Class 117 set No 424 (the 'L' now omitted) was used to break the official tape. With burnished buffer-heads and an appropriate notice on the front, the unit works out of Paddington as the 11.03 service to Maidenhead, one month later on 3 November. The buffers still show signs of the effort expended upon them, and the notice is still in position. Super glue?

Tyseley depot Class 117 three-car unit No T305 was specially painted into chocolate and cream livery for the 150th anniversary of the formation of the Great Western Railway in 1835. On 31 August 1991, the celebrity set was borrowed from Regional Railways Central by Thames Trains, to contrast with a new 'Thames Turbo' unit that was on view to the public for the day in Bourne End station. The Pressed Steel train was used as a Bourne End-Marlow shuttle and carried 'The Marlow Donkey' headboard, as well as the Tyseley depot 'bear in chains' logo on the old headcode box of DMS No 51410. The two-car Class 165/0 No 165005 provided the required contrast between 'ancient and modern'.

Minus the usual trailer, a newly-formed two-car Class 117 'power twin' unit No L724 departs from Ealing Broadway on 25 March 1992. DMBS No 51362 leads DMS No 51404 as the 14.37 Ealing Broadway to Greenford shuttle.

Already 9min late by the digital clock, the 19.09 service to Lichfield Trent Valley (one station on from Lichfield City, shown on the destination blind) is about to depart from Birmingham New Street station on 13 February 1993. The three-car Class 117 has its newly-applied unit number 117306 on show, and has been repainted from blue/grey into Regional Railways livery and fitted with a headlight. Whereas the previous livery was blue below the waistline with grey above it, this design is blue above the waist line, grey from the centre to the solebar, and has a light blue body stripe. DMS No 51411 leads downgraded trailer standard No 59521 and DMBS No 51369. All three vehicles were later transferred to ScotRail, working out of Haymarket depot.

Formed of Class 117 powercars Nos 51393 and 51351, the 12.40 Penzance-Plymouth train approaches Lostwithiel on 7 April 1993. Transferred to the West Country from Old Oak Common, the unit trailer car No 59503 was withdrawn in January 1993, and can now be seen on the Paignton & Dartmouth Railway. The now mandatory headlight is in place between the marker lights, and NSE livery is still worn.

Arriving at the newly-refurbished Harringay Green Lanes station (previously Harringay Stadium) on 7 December 1993, Class 117 'power twin' No L723 forms the 14.15 Gospel Oak-Barking train. The unit consists of DMS No 51399 and DMBS No 51361.

Two North London Railways Class 117 'power twins' were used for a commemorative train on 10 July 1994, to mark the centenary of the Barking-Gospel Oak line, the first services having operated to Southend-on-Sea in 1894. Units Nos L702/721 are unlikely visitors to the London, Tilbury & Southend Railway system, as they pass between Chalkwell and Leigh-on-Sea with empty stock of the special from Southend Central to Watford junction. The units returned from Watford to Southend Central in the evening, to pick up the passengers after a day at the seaside.

In Regional Railways colours, ScotRail three-car Pressed Steel unit No 117311 awaits departure time at Edinburgh Waverley on 24 August 1985. With headlight and marker lights shining, the unit forms the 07.25 'Fife Circle' service, out and back to Edinburgh via Cowdenbeath and Kirkcaldy. DMS No 51376 leads TSL No 59500 and DMBS No 51334.

Having satisfied the needs of the morning peak workings, two three-car Class 117 units depart from Edinburgh Waverley and head for Haymarket depot, where they are maintained. In the same way as the previous illustration, the leading DMS of unit No 117310, No 51415, is fitted with 'train to shore' radio transmission equipment, the fitting for which can now be clearly seen from this angle, situated on the roof behind the obsolete headcode box.

Two Pressed Steel Class 117 'power twins' operate the Clapham Junction-Willesden Junction 'Willy Belle' services at Kensington Olympia on 31 August 1995, unit No L707 heading for Clapham as the 17.13 from Willesden, and unit No L702 working the 17.14 from Clapham Junction in the opposite direction. Hammering through on the centre road, a Class 43 ex-DVT powercar No 43080 leads the 15.46 HST from Waterloo International to Manchester Piccadilly. This short-lived service was intended to whet the appetite of travellers in the north of England for future Regional Eurostar operations, but loadings remained obstinately very poor. *Ken Brunt*

'Ancient and modern' inside Bletchley Depot on 30 January 1996. Class 117 DMBS No 51350 entered traffic in June 1960. The Class 323 EMU alongside dates from 1992-3, but had only recently entered traffic following trials and modifications. One wonders if the '323' will still be in service in 36 years' time, in 2034?

Between the time that Class 455 EMUs operated the Clapham Junction-Kensington Olympia 'Kenny Belle' trains, and Class 313s took over for the extended Clapham Junction-Willesden Junction 'Willy Belle' services, diesel power was used again. Displaced on Paddington suburban services by 'Thames Turbos', some Class 117s were taken on by North London Railways (now Silverlink Passenger Trains) and used without trailer cars as 'power twins'. On 6 August 1996, DMS No 51396 leading DMBS No 51354 approaches Kensington Olympia as the 16.14 from Willesden Junction to Clapham junction, the leading vehicle having a non-standard '117' front end without the headcode box. This is the result of the work shown illustrated on page 141, the cab section of a withdrawn Class 116 replacing the damaged front of the Class 117.

Last days of DMUs on the Clapham Junction-Willesden Junction 'Willy Belle' services. With Class 313s due to take over from the start of the winter timetable, Class 117 vehicles Nos 51400 and 51358 cross the River Thames on Cremorne Viaduct, Chelsea Reach, forming the 17.37 from Willesden on 10 August 1996.

After transfer from 'Willy Belle' services to the Bedford-Bletchley 'Marston Vale' line, two Class 117 powercars were fitted with nameplates, the only 'Heritage' DMUs to receive names, apart from the Class 115 *Aylesbury College* in 1987. On 17 November 1996, DMBS No 51332 was named *Marston Vale* at Bedford Midland station by the Marchioness of Tavistock, to commemorate the 150th anniversary of the opening of the route. Afterwards, a presentation nameplate was given to her by railway staff in period costume.

At Bletchley station on 20 February 1997, Class 117 DMBS No 51358 was named after 'Mr Bedford-Bletchley', the ex-railwayman and activist for the route, *Leslie Crabbe*, who died suddenly a short time before. After the event, the newly-named vehicle headed a two-car special to Bedford, carrying many of his colleagues from the Bedford to Bletchley Rail Users' Association who attended to pay tribute. *(Below)* The nameplate unveiled by Leslie Crabbe's brother, Gerry Crabbe.

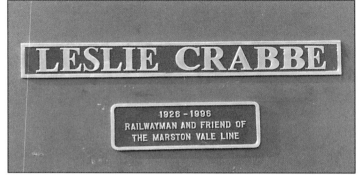

In typical 'Marston Vale' surroundings, near Ridgmont, the 11.40 train from Bedford Midland to Bletchley is formed of Class 117 'power twin' No L707, augmented by Class 121 single-car unit No 55027. Shortly afterwards, the 'bubblecar' was stored by North London Railways as spare to its operating requirements, but was later taken on by Great Eastern Railways, with two others, to work the Colchester-Sudbury line until a Class 153 could be returned.

Stabled in Exeter St Davids station yard after being withdrawn from South Wales & West Railway duties on the Cornish branch lines, ex-Penzance depot Class 117 units Nos 305, 708 and 709 await an uncertain future on 24 May 1997. Alongside, in the claret and yellow colours of English, Welsh & Scottish Railway, is Class 37/7 No 37707.

Birmingham RC&W three-car Class 118

Built by:	Birmingham Railway Carriage & Wagon Company
Introduced:	April 1960
Coupling Code:	Blue Square ■
Engines in each Driving Motor:	Two BUT (Leyland) six-cylinder horizontal type 150hp
Transmission:	Mechanical, Standard
Body:	64ft 0in x 9ft 3in
Weight:	DMBS 36 tons
	DMS 36 tons
	TCL 30 tons
Operating numbers:	DMBS 51302 to 51316
	DMS 51317 to 51331
	TCL 59469 to 59483

A total of 15 three-car Birmingham RC&W high-density suburban units was ordered as an add-on to the Class 116 and Class 117 fleets built by BR Derby Works and the Pressed Steel Company, respectively, and were constructed to the standard Derby design of the period. Manufactured at Smethwick, Staffordshire, from April to July 1960, they were built quickly for a Western Region requirement, and like their counterparts were designed without gangways between the cars in each set. In the same way as the Class 117s, the trailer composite vehicles had two lavatory compartments, but these could not be used by passengers travelling in either the front or rear car. Following 'representations' from passengers on long journeys in the non-gangwayed driving cars, connecting facilities were installed. Withdrawal of the class commenced in 1987, but was not completed until 1994-5, driving motors Nos 51314 and 51329 being the last to go from Tyseley depot. DMS No 51321 is preserved on the Battlefield Line. The original TOPS classifications for the three types of vehicle were:

118/1	Driving Motor Second
118/2	Driving Motor Brake Second
174	Trailer Composite with lavatory

New to traffic in May 1960, a three-car BRC&W suburban DMU passes between Teignmouth and Newton Abbot on 8 July 1960, forming the 17.44 local service from Exeter to Newton Abbot. DMBS No W51308 leads TCL No W59475 and DMS No W51323. Painted in dark Brunswick green, with cream lining, white cab roof canopy and 'speed whiskers', only the marker lights below the cab windows, fitted from new, betray that this is not a Pressed Steel Company Class 117, which otherwise looks identical. *Peter W. Gray*

During the early 1960s, Plymouth Laira-based BRC&W units often ran without the trailer vehicle, depriving passengers of any toilet facility. Comprised of the two driving motors, DMS No W51319 leads a Plymouth-bound local service on 3 May 1961, approaching Keyham. The driving motor brake vehicles had 65 second class seats, and the driving motors without a brake compartment had provision for 91. Only the trailers were composite vehicles, having 24 seats for first class ticket holders and 50 for 'seconds'. *R. C. Riley*

Passing St Dennis Junction, another two-car BRC&W 'power twin' heads for Par on 21 June 1962, forming a branch service from Newquay. It is likely at this stage that the trailer was in the process of being modified with gangway connections. *R. C. Riley*

Snorting up the 1 in 37 climb from Exeter St Davids to Exeter Central on 21 July 1977, what is now classified as a 118 unit No P473, forms the 14.47 local service from St Davids to Exmouth. Class 118/2 DMBS No W51316 leads, and with the remainder of the set, is now in unlined plain blue livery with yellow ends. The roof-mounted route indicator panel has been blanked off, the blue square coupling code has been painted out, and the 'lion and wheel' emblem changed for the 'BR arrow'.

With the original side lights below the driving windows removed and replaced with two marker lights cut into the otherwise out of use route indicator box, DMS No W51318 leads Class 118 unit No P461, approaching Newton Abbot on 2 July 1979, as a local service from Paignton. The 'P' prefix to the unit number shows that its allocation is Plymouth Laira.

Formed of a three-car Class 118 unit leading a Metro-Cammell three-car Class 101, the 16.57 train from Bristol Temple Meads to Cardiff Central restarts from the Severn Tunnel Junction stop on 15 September 1979. Driving motor No W51324 leads Bristol Bath Road-based unit No B467. Another example of marker lights in the headcode box replacing those below the driving windows, a scheme that was quickly discontinued and the headcode boxes were then blacked out.

With the yellow band above the four first class compartments readily visible from this angle, DMS No W51325 leads Bristol unit No B468, forming the 15.30 train from Cheltenham Spa to Swindon, approaching Stonehouse. The headcode box has been painted to match the roof panels, and marker lights are fitted in the original position below the cab windows.

The noon departure from Gunnislake for Plymouth approaches Calstock on 5 July 1980, running above the town before winding round into the station. With the trailer removed, the '118' 'power twin' is formed of DMBS No W51312 leading DMS No W51327.

Running nonstop through the now closed halt of Radipole, Bristol-based Class 118 unit No B472 forms the 13.00 service from Weymouth to Bristol Temple Meads on 27 November 1982. Driving motor No W51330 leads the standard three-car formation. Although not included in the refurbishment plan, the '118' fleet was smartened up during the 1980s by the provision of 'Inter-City' blue and grey livery.

Having been constructed to follow the course of the River Taw, the Barnstaple line is required to bridge the waters a number of times before reaching its destination. On 19 September 1983, Class 118 motor brake No W51313 of set No P470 crosses the river, near Chapelton, forming the 18.27 'stopper' from Barnstaple to Exeter St Davids.

With motor brake No W51307 leading, Class 118 set No P465 approaches Exeter Central station on 23 July 1985, forming the 09.48 local service from Exmouth to Exeter St Davids. The graffiti that has begun to appear on the brickwork of the signalbox almost covered it before the building was demolished.

In 1986, Class 118 sets from the West Country were being replaced (short term as it happened) by the then new Class 142 'Skipper' units. Some BRC&W sets were transferred to Cardiff Canton for use on South Wales suburban duties and were given some parochial treatment by the addition of the Welsh dragon and the words 'Trên y Cwm' on one side of each car and the translation *(Below)* 'Valley Train' on the other. With rather thin-looking 'speed whiskers' and the trailer removed, set No C470 moves off from Newport as an empty coaching stock movement on 2 October 1986, having arrived as a local service from Swansea. DMS No W51328 leads DMBS No W51313.

In February 1985, Plymouth Laira-allocated '118' unit No P460 was painted into British Telecom yellow livery for advertising purposes, and made its debut with a special promotional run from Exeter to Liskeard. With the DMBS No 51302 bearing the slogan 'it's the TELECOM on the line' on one side and 'working fast connections' on the other, the train passes Powderham on 6 July 1987, forming the 10.10 from Exeter St Davids to Paignton. The vehicle number is unusually carried below the driver's side window.
Colin J. Marsden

With 'Westbury' displayed in the destination blind, Bristol Bath Road-allocated Class 118 set No B473 passes Fairwood Junction on 16 April 1986, forming the 13.05 train from Weymouth to Westbury. Driving Motor No W51331 is leading.

Few complete three-car Class 118 units remained by 1987, rapid inroads having been made into them by the arrival of what were then new Class 150 'Sprinters'. Having just passed through the Cardiff Canton depot carriage washing plant, set No C480 consists of vehicles Nos W51312, W59479 and W51327. Displaying a 'Hereford' destination, the unit is passed by Class 08 No 08664, which is shunting stock.

As the remaining Class 118s approached the end of their life, any form of major repair was ruled out and individual vehicles were withdrawn from service, leaving odd cars still to ply their trade, often attached to other types having a similar fate. Driving motor No 51319 was one example, transferred to Reading depot and attached to Class 116 motor brake No 53820 to operate the north London Gospel Oak-Barking line. Both vehicles were surprisingly painted into the red, white, blue and grey colours of Network SouthEast, and are seen passing Harringay Park Junction signalbox on 17 February 1989, as the 12.30 from Barking to Gospel Oak. Given a London unit number L705, it is also fitted with a new white-on-blue destination blind.

Gloucester RC&W three-car Class 119

Built by:	Gloucester Railway Carriage & Wagon Company
Introduced:	October 1958
Coupling Code:	Blue Square ■
Engines in each Driving Motor:	Two BUT (AEC)or Leyland six-cylinder horizontal type 150hp
Transmission:	Mechanical, Standard
Body:	64ft 6in x 9ft 3in

Weight:	DMBC	36 tons 19cwt
	DMSL	37 tons 10cwt
	TBSL	31 tons 8cwt
Operating numbers:	DMBC	51052 to 51079
	DMSL	51080 to 51107
	TBSL	59413 to 59437

British Rail's Modernisation Plan of 1955 recognised that there was a need for a special type of diesel multiple-unit to operate the numerous cross-country routes which then still figured quite largely on the railway map. As some journeys were quite lengthy, provision of a buffet car facility seemed justified, and seating needed to be at least as comfortable as the locomotive-hauled stock they were to replace. In this case, passenger comfort was required to be of a standard above any competing road vehicle, not just equivalent to it. Gloucester RC&W was approached and agreed to construct 28 three-car cross-country units to BR Derby specifications, rather than to its own railcar design introduced in 1957 that became the Class 100 units. A large guard's compartment

was incorporated in the motor brakes on the new trains, and the trailer second vehicles had a small buffet area, seating just four people. Gangways were fitted within each three-car formation. Apart from accident damage, the first withdrawals came about in the late 1980s, the last examples, allocated to Tyseley depot, lasting until 1995. Three powercars have been preserved, two on the Pontypool & Blaenavon Railway and one on the Mid-Norfolk.

Original TOPS classifications for the three types of vehicle were:

119/1	Driving Motor Brake Composite
119/2	Driving Motor Second with lavatory
178	Trailer Buffet Second with lavatory

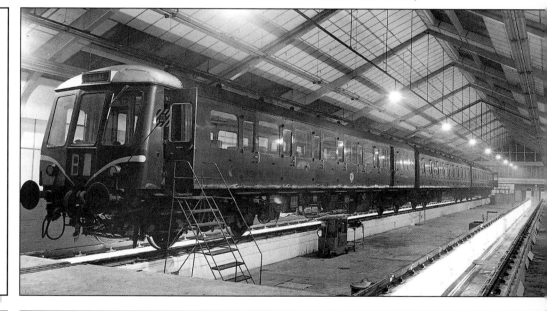

The first GRC&W cross-country unit was delivered to Marsh Junction depot, Bristol, and photographed there for official purposes on 20 May 1959, while under routine maintenance. The unit is in original malachite green livery with yellow lining and 'speed whiskers', and a white fibreglass cab roof canopy that incorporates the destination blind. In order not to cut across the two-panel route indicators, the 'speed whiskers' do not meet at the base of the 'V' in the usual way. *British Railways*

It was not envisaged that passengers on the stopping service between Severn Beach and Bristol Temple Meads would be in need of buffet facilities, even allowing for the fact that this train is routed via Pilning, in the days before Severn Beach became a reluctant branch line terminus. However, on 29 September 1959, less than seven months after introduction, GRC&W cross-country DMBC No W51062 leads trailer buffet No W59420 and motor second No W51089 as the 14.30 from Severn Beach. The unit is arriving at New Passage Halt. *Michael Mensing*

On 6 September 1961, two three-car cross-country DMUs are merged to form the 08.30 Carmarthen-Bristol Temple Meads train, entering the temporary station erected at Port Talbot while work proceeds on the main platforms. The leading Gloucester set is formed of DMSL No W51083, TBSL No W59417 and DMBC No W51055. The second unit is a BR Swindon unit, later to be classified 120. *John N. Faulkner*

On 15 April 1963, a GRC&W cross-country unit is used for the Yeovil Town-Yeovil Pen Mill shuttle service. DMSL No W51094 leads TBSL No W59425 and DMBC No W51066. The unit retains its original malachite green livery, but now displays a half-yellow front warning panel, replacing the original 'speed whiskers'. As the original white cab roof panels became very dirty in service, they were painted over to match the rest of the roof. *John N. Faulkner*

During the transition period from steam to diesel traction in the early 1960s, and prior to the full complement of DMUs being built, three Hawksworth GWR corridor composite coaches, Nos W7254W, W7804W and W7813W, were converted at Swindon works to allow them to be marshalled within DMU sets. This was to strengthen three-car units to four-cars when required. They were used mainly with cross-country units, but were also utilised occasionally on some Western Region suburban duties from Paddington. The vehicles were painted in green with cream lining to match the DMU stock and were fitted with DMU jumper cables. Also, the brakes were modified, and lighting circuits altered to work with DMU batteries. On 10 June 1963, the third vehicle of a seven-car Class 119 unit passing near Twyford is one of the ex-steam-hauled coaches, all three of which were withdrawn from traffic in March 1967. Led by DMSL No W51098, the train is probably a Paddington-Oxford service. *Colin J. Marsden collection*

Heading away from Westbury, a GRC&W three-car unit forms a Cardiff Central-Weymouth Town service on 13 July 1964, an appropriate working for a cross-country DMU. DMSL No W51097 is nearest to the camera, and although still retaining 'speed whiskers' at this stage, the white cab roof panel has already been painted over. A GWR pannier tank can just be seen in the distance shunting tank wagons. *R. C. Riley*

Forming a train from Bradford to Leeds, a GRC&W Class 119 unit, attached to a Metro-Cammell Class 101 set, approaches its destination on a summer day in 1965. Travelling in the opposite direction, 'Britannia' Pacific No 70046 (once named *Anzac*) departs from Leeds with a vans train for Carlisle. *Les Nixon*

The closure of many routes for which cross-country units were designed, resulted in their appearance on inappropriate trains. On 8 July 1976, Plymouth Laira-based Class 119 set No P577 departs from St Ives as the 13.59 to St Erth, a journey time of under 15min. Despite the destination blind showing 'Excursion', this is a service train. Now in blue/grey livery with full-yellow end, Class 119/2 No W51091 is nearest to the camera. The route indicator panel on the vehicle has been removed without trace, and the mandatory red lamp is carried.

On a misty 26 March 1977, Bristol-allocated Class 119 unit No B575 departs from Westbury, forming the 08.48 train from Portsmouth Harbour to Bristol Temple Meads. Class 119/2 DMSL No W51088 is leading a six-car formation. The route indicator and destination blind frames are still fitted, but both appear to be out of use. Westbury signalbox and attendant semaphore signals have all since disappeared.

The 09.45 Sunday service from Bristol Temple Meads to Cardiff Central departs from the Severn Tunnel Junction stop on 16 September 1979 and passes the yards of the same name. The three-car Class 119 unit No B571 is headed by brake composite No W51052, the first powercar of the type to emerge from the Gloucester RC&W works in October 1958. In the yards can be seen two Class 20s, a Class 25, a Class 31, two Class 45 'Peaks' and a Class 47, all stabled there until the Monday morning.

Driving brake composite No W51074 leads three-car Class 119 set No C595 on 12 April 1980, forming the 13.00 train from Newport to Gloucester. The unit is crossing the bridge over the River Wye at Chepstow. This was originally built by Brunel in 1852, but in 1962 it was reconstructed with the train deck supported from beneath by lattice girders. Today, the view has changed yet again, with the A48 Chepstow bypass road running alongside.

In a typical Cornish setting, the noon train from Bodmin Road sets out for Plymouth on 2 July 1980, formed of Gloucester RC&W Class 119 set No P594. As can clearly be seen from this angle, each low density car has two doors. The motor brake No W51073 on the rear carries 18 first class seats and 16 standard class. The trailer No W59435 has provision for 60 in standard class, and the leading driving motor standard seats 68. The clips at cant-rail level were provided for side destination boards, but do not seem to have been used, even in the early days.

In 1981-2, the large guard's vans in the DMBC vehicles of most Class 119s were converted for use as passenger luggage stowage areas, together with the buffet areas in the trailer cars which had been out of use for some years. The units with increased luggage space were then concentrated on Reading-Gatwick Airport services and allocated to Reading depot. On 28 April 1982, a converted Gloucester RC&W set No L581, with DMSL No W51095 leading, passes between Redhill and Earlswood, working the 08.15 service from Reading to Gatwick Airport.

Class 119 motor brake and trailers converted for Gatwick Express Airport services received a white-on-red painted notice on the bodysides. The trailer cars were reclassified as luggage trailer seconds.

Passenger Luggage Stowage Area

Class 119 set No 594 works the 12.44 train from Hereford to Birmingham New Street on 21 September 1982 and tops the 1 in 37 of the Lickey incline, with driving motor No W51104 leading. At this time, the unit was allocated to Reading depot and remained there another 12 years. The prefix 'L' has been painted out as if it was to be permanently transferred to another depot, possibly Tyseley, but a permanent move to the Midlands did not take place for No 51104 until 1994!

Two Gloucester Class 119 three-car cross-country sets provide an unlikely sight approaching Clapham Junction on 14 May 1983. The rear unit No L581, nearest to the camera, has been repainted and labelled up for Reading-Gatwick Airport services, but the leading one has not. Showing 'Special' on the destination blind, the rear car is DMSL No W51095. A rear oil lamp no longer needs to be carried, as electric tail lights are now incorporated in the marker light housings.

The 13.10 cross-country service from Westbury to Weymouth passes Witham Friary, south of Frome, on 16 September 1983, formed of Class 119 set No B596, with DMSL No W51099 leading. Observe the difference in the appearance of the trailer car compared with the one shown in other illustrations. The two sides vary, as the window position behind the former buffet on one side only is plated over.

On a cold and wet 6 February 1984, a standard Class 119 Gatwick Airport three-car unit No L594 rasps away from the airport on time at 12.07, and heads for Reading. To the rear, a Class 423 4VEP EMU is in the platform, forming a service to Horsham.

Class 119 units converted for extra luggage space were also used on the cross-country Reading-Tonbridge trains, as well as the semi-fast services extending to Gatwick Airport. With the dilapidated corrugated iron platform shelter at Betchworth looking more suitable for local vagrants than train passengers, Gloucester '119' unit No L575 enters the station on 28 May 1984 as the 16.52 train from Tonbridge to Reading. DMSL No W51088 is leading.

On the Great Western main line between Tilehurst and Pangbourne, Gloucester cross-country set No B590 has been 'borrowed' from Bristol Bath Road depot and operates the 16.37 Oxford to Paddington train on 14 June 1985. DMSL No W51087 is leading.

The 13.42 Didcot Parkway-Paddington train and the 14.35 Paddington-Plymouth relief pass near Langley on 22 April 1987, with a local service from Paddington to Maidenhead also visible in the distance. The InterCity service is headed by Class 50 No 50029 *Renown*, and the London-bound DMU is formed of Gloucester cross-country set No L596, with motor brake No W51076 nearest to the camera.

Having worked the Clapham Junction-Kensington Olympia morning services on 22 January 1988, a grubby GRC&W cross-country set No L576 heads for Redhill, from where it will operate off-peak Redhill-Reading trains until returning to Clapham Junction again for the evening peak services to Olympia. Passing Calvert Road Junction, in south-west London, the leading motor brake, No W51062, displays a Network SouthEast logo below the centre cab window, in addition to some unsightly graffiti on the bodyside.

Although it was destined to be withdrawn from service in only six months' time, Class 119 motor brake No 51058 has been fitted with a new headlight, and coupled to Class 101 DMSL No 53235 forms two-car hybrid unit No C590 on 24 February 1988. As the 'C' prefix on the front indicates that the vehicles are allocated to Cardiff Canton depot, it is strange to see the unit at Middlesbrough, diagrammed for the 12.30 Darlington-Saltburn train! In the other platform, Class 143 'Pacer' No 143002 forms the 13.03 service from Middlesbrough to Newcastle.

The 12.20 Reading-Redhill 'North Downs Line' train departs from the Wokingham stop on 15 March 1992, formed of one of the six complete Class 119 DMUs then remaining in service. Now in full Network SouthEast (NSE) livery, unit No L596 is led by driving brake No 51076, regional number prefixes no longer being in use.

On 18 February 1993, Class 119 powercars Nos 51088 and 51060 await departure time at Wolverhampton, forming the 11.25 train to Shrewsbury. Now allocated to Tyseley, unit No T575 has received a unique livery, the red, white, blue and grey of NSE having been amended by the expedient of painting the red stripe dark blue. *Michael Oakley*

As already mentioned, problems with the introduction of new Class 323 EMUs resulted in the Birmingham Cross-City services in the mid-1990s having to resort to a number of older units, including this hybrid DMU set which was literally on its 'last knockings'. On 25 June 1994, two Class 119 driving motors in NSE colours lead a Class 116 power-car, to form the 12.24 Redditch-Lichfield Trent Valley train. With its headlight in place, DMSL No 51107 leads the formation passing Shenstone. This car was the last of the type to be built at Gloucester, in January 1960.

BR Swindon 'Cross-country' two-car Class 120

Built by:	British Rail Swindon Works
Introduced:	October 1957
Coupling Code:	Blue Square ■
Engines in each Driving Motor:	Two BUT (AEC), or Leyland, six-cylinder horizontal type 150hp
Transmission:	Mechanical, Standard
Body:	64ft 6in x 9ft 3in
Weight:	DMBCL	36 tons 7cwt
	DMSL	36 tons 10cwt
	DMBF	36 tons 0cwt
	TBSL	31 tons 8cwt
	TSL	30 tons 12cwt
Operating numbers:	DMBCL	50696 to 50744, 51573 to 51581, 51781/2/7
	DMSL	50647 to 50695, 51582 to 51590, 51788 to 51794
	DMBF	51783 to 51786
	TBSL	59255 to 59301, 59679 to 59685
	TSL	59579 to 59588
Renumbered:	All surviving cars in 50xxx series renumbered to 53xxx in 1980-1.

Constructed between 1957 and 1960, the 130 powercars and 64 trailers built at Swindon works for cross-country use were formed mainly into three-car sets, although 11 vehicles for Western Region began their life as two-car units. Internally, all were similar to the later Gloucester RC&W Class 119s, but externally they strongly resembled the BR Swindon Inter-City units built in 1956. At first, there were three different types of driving motor, the usual second class vehicle, a composite brake and a first class-only brake with the second class seating used for additional luggage space. In addition, there were 54 centre trailers containing a small buffet area with four wall seats, and another ten constructed later without a refreshment facility. The first train entered revenue-earning service in March 1958 between Birmingham and South Wales, displacing diagrams previously operated by steam, or by the earlier Inter-City diesel sets. In the same way as the Class 119s, Beeching line closures put paid to many cross-country routes and as a result some units were moved around from area to area, often finishing up on services for which they were never intended. Three driving motors and five trailers were withdrawn after accident damage. Apart from these, the fleet remained operational until 1982, when some trailers were taken out of service. Powercars followed from 1984, the last four being sold to MC Metal Processing, Glasgow, for breaking up in October 1989. Eight driving motors were stripped out at Chester for use as parcels vehicles in March 1987, but were withdrawn just two months later, having been found superfluous to requirements. One trailer, No M59276, is preserved at the Great Central Railway, Loughborough, where it operates with two Class 127 power cars. The first TOPS classifications for the vehicles were:

120/1	Driving Motor Brake Composite with lavatory
	Driving Motor Brake First with lavatory
120/2	Driving Motor Second with lavatory
179	Trailer Buffet Second with lavatory
	Trailer Second with lavatory

Forming the 15.05 service for Cardiff Central, a BR Swindon three-car cross-country unit climbs away from Shrewsbury on 24 September 1960, and passes Bayston Hill. It is in original dark Brunswick green livery, with cream lining and 'speed whiskers', and driving motor second No W50662 is leading. *Michael Mensing*

On 31 January 1959, BR Swindon motor brake No W50697 is turned on the Cardiff Canton steam locomotive turntable. This was normal practice at the time by the adjacent diesel depot staff when reforming diesel sets after maintenance or repair. The vehicle is fitted with four marker lights and a destination blind above the cab windows. *Bob Tuck*

Having emerged brand-new from Swindon works, cross-country motor brake No W50718 heads a two-car test run on 14 April 1958. The four-figure route indicator panel fitted could well be under evaluation here, as later examples emerged from Swindon without the facility, which was not introduced until 1961. In addition, vehicles built with the front panel retained only two side marker lights, whereas this one still has all four. The 'Blue Square' coupling code signs are clearly shown above the buffers. *Colin J. Marsden collection*

Photographed from atop the old Exeter St Davids water tower, a Swindon cross-country unit from Kingswear arrives at its destination on 2 July 1963, headed by DMSL No W51585, with route indicator panel and two side marker lights only. TBSL No W59262 forms the second vehicle. White cab roof panels were popular at this time, but their regard quickly diminished when it was realised just how dirty they became in traffic. *R. C. Riley*

Interior of a BR Swindon-built cross-country second class saloon when new. The original upholstery is in shades of green, with cream leatherette headrests. In the early years, even second class had curtains, and passengers wore furs and read the *Tatler* magazine! *Ian Allan Library*

Newly painted into what was then known as 'Inter-City' livery, a Swindon cross-country unit in blue and grey crosses the River Taw at Barnstaple on 12 August 1968. Formed of DMSL No W51586, TBSL No W59683 and DMBC No W51577, the train is the 08.10 from Ilfracombe to Exeter St Davids. The motor brake second vehicles seated 68, the motor brake composites had seats for 18 in first class and 16 in 'second', and the trailer buffet seconds provided 60 normal seats and a further four wall seats in the buffet area. *Maurice Edwards*

Formed of a three-car BR Swindon cross-country unit, the 14.38 Kidderminster-Hereford train crosses to the single line section through Ledbury tunnel on 24 June 1964. 'Speed whiskers' have given way to a half-yellow front-end panel, and it can be seen how the white cab roof canopy became dirtied in traffic. *Ben Ashworth*

In overall BR 'corporate blue' livery, one of the four Class 120/1 driving motor brake first cars, No Sc51783, leads the 10.35 service from Aberdeen to Inverness on 27 March 1974, climbing towards Kittybrewster. The figure '1' is painted onto the single passenger door, and to emphasise its first-only facility, a yellow stripe is evident above the first class compartments at cant-rail level. The original second class seating has been removed to facilitate a large luggage area. Automatic tablet exchange equipment was fitted to the seven units allocated to Scottish Region for these duties, and can be seen at the rear of the first vehicle.

A BR Swindon Class 120 cross-country unit departs under the wires from a rainy Kidsgrove station on 17 April 1975, forming the 11.20 train from Crewe to Lincoln. The red tail lamp securely in place is the fifth lighting facility on this end of the unit, although it is doubtful if more than one or two of the lower marker lights is operational at this stage. *Philip D. Hawkins, FGRA*

Fuelling up outside Lochgorm works, Inverness, on 31 March 1976, unit No 305 stands alongside Class 26/2 No 26045. The Class 120 cross-country set consists of motor composite No Sc51793, trailer buffet second No Sc59684 and motor brake first No Sc51786. The word 'Buffet' is still evident on the centre car, although such a facility was comparatively rare at this time and the serving area was normally locked.

Departing from the Umberleigh stop, and passing milepost 204¾, Plymouth Laira-allocated Class 120 set No P554 forms the 11.00 service from Exmouth to Barnstaple on 14 July 1976. Powercars Nos W51575 and W51584 sandwich a blue-liveried Class 174 (118) trailer composite. The nearest car has its route indicator panel plated over and marker lights inserted, but is still required to carry a tail light.

Arriving at Falmouth on 14 July 1977, three-car Swindon Class 120 set No 557 is augmented by a blue-liveried Class 121 single car unit No W55026. With driving motor No W51587 leading, return to Truro is timed for 13.49. On this vehicle, the original route indicator panel has been plated over, but the original marker lights are retained.

Passing camping coaches, the 07.45 Cardiff Central to Pembroke Dock train arrives at Tenby on 5 September 1979. The two-car Cardiff Canton-based Class 120 unit No C602 is formed of DMBC No W50698 and DMSL No W50649. The headlight fitted below the disused destination blind panel is a powerful one for use when operating over the Central Wales line. *Chris Perkins*

With its headlight aglow, Class 120 two-car unit No C604 emerges from Sugar Loaf tunnel, between Cynghordy and Llanwrtyd, on 10 September 1979, forming the 09.59 Central Wales Line train from Swansea to Shrewsbury. Driving motor second No W50681 leads motor brake No W50701. The tunnel once marked the old border between Carmarthenshire and Brecknockshire.

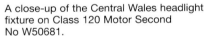

A close-up of the Central Wales headlight fixture on Class 120 Motor Second No W50681.

Formed of Class 120 DMBC No W50705, TSL No W59588 and DMSL No W50665, the 11.15 train from Swansea to Milford Haven approaches its destination on 11 September 1979. At the time, the Class 179 trailer vehicle was one of only ten without a buffet facility, and seated 68 in second class instead of 60 plus four wall seats in the buffet area.

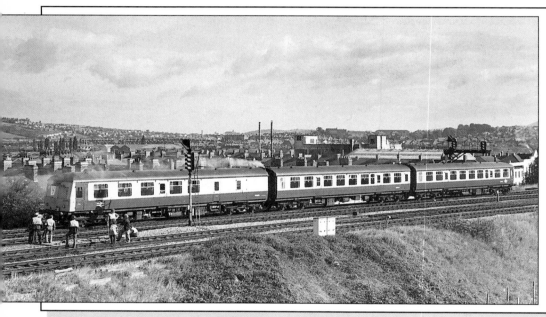

A track maintenance team stand aside as Class 120 cross-country Set No C558 departs from Newport and approaches Maindee West Junction on 14 September 1979, heading for Birmingham New Street. This view clearly shows the make-up of the three cars; the brake composite No W51579 is at the rear, the centre car is ex-buffet trailer second No W59264, and leading is motor second No W51588. The complete unit has seven passenger doors on each side.

Entering Elgin station on 23 January 1980, three-car Swindon cross-country unit No 304 is augmented on the rear by a Gloucester RC&W Class 122 single car No Sc55011. With motor second No Sc51790 leading, the train is the 11.55 from Aberdeen to Inverness. When locomotive-hauled trains took over the Aberdeen-Inverness services later in 1980, the seven Class 120 Swindon sets allocated to Inverness were transferred away, four going to Cardiff and three to Ayr, where they lasted under a year before moving on again to Derby Etches Park depot.

As already mentioned, three of the original Inverness-based Class 120 units were transferred to Ayr depot in 1980, but their tenure was short-lived, all being reallocated to Derby in the following year. On 28 August 1980, motor brake No Sc51787 leads two Class 101 Metro Cammell vehicles, approaching Drumlanrigg tunnel as the 09.00 train from Ayr to Carlisle. Although some Class 120 units were included in the BR refurbishment programme, it became evident after the first two had been completely stripped of blue asbestos insulation, reconditioned and re-upholstered, that major attention of this nature was very costly. As a result, only superficial improvements were carried out on others of the type, and meant that the days of the 1957-built Swindon 'cross-countrys' were now numbered. None received the first refurbishment livery of off-white with a blue stripe, as applied to the rear car. *Les Nixon*

A Central Wales train sets out on its journey from Shrewsbury to Swansea on 14 September 1981, formed of BR Swindon Class 120 'power twin' set No C601 with driving motor No M50722 leading No 50672. With a possibility of having to call at all 31 stations en route, the journey time to Swansea is over 3½hr.

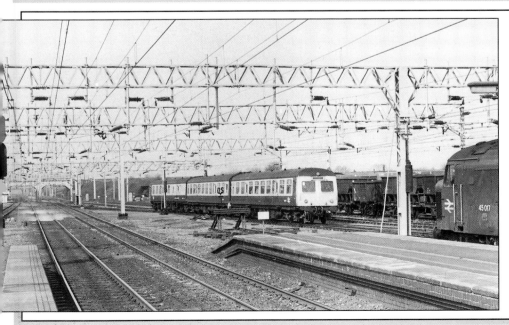

On 27 March 1982, a Class 120 unit arrives at Nuneaton as the 11.17 Saturday service from Birmingham New Street to Leicester, with DMSL No M50687 leading. The motor second vehicles had provision for seating 68 in second class, with the motor brake composites accommodating 18 in first class and 16 in standard. Already in the platform is Class 45/0 'Peak' No 45017, waiting for a clear road with a northbound special charter.

A more unsuitable task for a cross-country unit could hardly be imagined than operating the two-and-a-half-mile Sinfin branch! Departing from Sinfin Central terminus on 1 July 1983, a three-car BR Swindon Class 120 unit forms the 08.01 to Derby, completely lacking any passengers. From Derby, the unit was then diagrammed for a slightly more appropriate service to Matlock. To avoid a clash with locomotive and unit numbers on the BR TOPS computer, the original M50708 number on the leading motor brake has been changed to No M53708. So few passengers used the Sinfin trains, that after the demise of the 'Heritage' DMUs, the 'train' became a taxi. Even this was withdrawn in June 1998.

Passing the old Threlfalls brewery buildings at Deal Street Junction, a three-car Swindon Class 120 unit and a two-car Birmingham RC&W Class 104, still in blue, approach Manchester Victoria on 31 May 1984. The five vehicles are led by DMSL No M51793 and form the 18.15 service from Blackpool North.

The new year of 1986 saw the East Midlands network transformed into what folk thought would be the bright new world of 'Sprinters'. The Etches Park Class 120s were dispersed in all directions and some powercars found their way north of the border again to supplement the Scottish DMU fleet, until ScotRail's own 'Sprinters' came on stream and the Ayr line electrification was completed. On 30 May 1988, three of the last examples of the Swindon cross-countrys remaining in service pass the site of Bo'ness Junction, mixed with Metro-Cammell Class 101 vehicles and forming the 15.10 train from Edinburgh Waverley to Dunblane. The six-car unit is headed by downgraded Class 120 motor standard vehicle No 53699, followed by Metro-Cammell Class 101 TSL No 59571 and Swindon DMS No 53658. Then follows another '120' DMBS No 53733, and two further '101' cars, TSL No 59065 and DMBS No 53215.

Replaced on Kilmarnock and East Kilbride services by Metro-Cammell Class 156 'Sprinter' units, the last examples of BR Swindon-built cross-country Class 120 DMU was finally withdrawn from service in September 1989, bowing out quietly as there was no apparent interest from preservationists. On what could well have been its last revenue-earning diagram, DMSL No 53658 heads the 16.24 to East Kilbride at Glasgow Central on 28 September 1989, only the backplate of its top marker light remaining. Alongside is Class 101 unit No 101321, the DMBS No 51249 leading the 16.15 train for Barrhead.

Pressed Steel Company single unit Railcar Class 121

Built by:	Pressed Steel Company, Linwood, Scotland
Introduced:	September 1960
Coupling Code:	Blue Square ■
Engines in each Driving Motor:	Two BUT (AEC) or Leyland six-cylinder horizontal type 150hp
Transmission:	Mechanical, Standard
Body:	64ft 6in x 9ft 3in
Weight:	DMBS 37 tons
	DTS 29 tons
Operating numbers:	DMBS 55020 to 55035
	DTS 56280 to 56289

Constructed to the standard BR Derby high-density design for general branch line and local services, the Pressed Steel single unit railcars were considered as the BR equivalent of the original GWR AEC single railcars. They were powerful enough to haul other vehicles and could work in multiple with them if required to do so. The 16 single cars were delivered with 10 non-powered driving trailer seconds to work with them, but these had a driving cab at one end only, which meant that the powercar had to be coupled to the 'dumb' end if used. From the beginning, the units were allocated to the Western Region, and were used on Cornish branch line services and other minor lines emanating from London and Bristol. One, No W55035, was withdrawn from passenger service as early as 1978 and transferred to Departmental stock as a route learning vehicle No ADB 975659. The remainder were included in the refurbishment programme, and the majority survive both on passenger services and in Departmental use, although the driving trailers were all withdrawn from passenger service by 1992. As late as 1998, three units stored by Silverlink Trains were returned to passenger use to operate the Great Eastern Railway's Marks Tey-Sudbury branch, until the Class 153 operated by Anglia Railways could be returned again. Currently seven '121s' are working as 'Sandite' application vehicles for Railtrack, and others are already in preservation, with more certain to be taken on. Currently Mangapps Farm Railway Museum, the Battlefield Line, and the Chinnor & Princes Risborough, Colne Valley, Gloucestershire Warwickshire, and Swansea Vale Railways all have examples.

BR TOPS computer classification was 121, with the trailers given Class 149.

The Pressed Steel single unit railcars were introduced in dark Brunswick green livery with 'speed whiskers', which were eventually substituted by a half-yellow front panel. In original condition, after entering service in October the previous year, No W55027 forms the 15.36 train from Didcot to Newbury on 22 September 1961, and heads through the countryside south of Didcot. *Michael Mensing*

Now sporting the half-yellow front and looking particularly smart with a light-grey roof to nearly match the cab roof canopy, No W55026 passes near Milverton on 23 June 1965, forming the 11.10 train from Taunton to what was then Barnstaple Junction. *Michael Mensing*

When the 65 seats in a Pressed Steel Company single unit railcar were likely to be insufficient for demand, one of the 10 driving trailer second vehicles built at the same time could be attached. On Good Friday, 16 April 1965, motor brake No W55020 passes Moreton, east of Didcot, leading the 17.55 service from Reading to Oxford. The off-white roof of the powercar has not been given to its attendant 95-seater trailer. *Michael Mensing*

Showing the exhaust system fitted to one end only, Class 121 car No W55021 stands in Southall depot yard on 20 March 1976, between duties on the Greenford branch. It now has all-over blue paintwork with a full-yellow front end, and the four-character headcode box is redundant, displaying four noughts prior to being blanked off altogether. To accommodate the box at roof level, the arrangement of the exhaust stacks is such as to resemble antlers. In addition to the car number, a unit number L121, is also shown below the driving cab window.

As single-car vehicles, the Classes 121 and 122 railcars were given the nickname 'bubblecars', a sobriquet which became generally used by both professional railwaymen and enthusiasts alike. On 29 August 1989, No W55033 approaches Clifton Down while working the 12.22 service from Avonmouth to Bristol Temple Meads. The roof-mounted headcode box is now painted over. *Barry J. Nicolle*

With Pressed Steel '121' No W55023 leading Class 149 driving trailer No W56281, the 11.39 shuttle from Marlow to Maidenhead runs between Marlow and Bourne End on 27 May 1981, where the train is required to reverse. Both vehicles are now painted into the much more attractive blue/grey livery.

Having arrived at Bourne End, direction of the train is reversed and the driving trailer will now lead to Maidenhead. As there were fewer trailer cars than there were powercars, they tended to be coupled and uncoupled as required. As a result, they received their own unit numbers, this one showing L281.

Ideally suited to the Looe branch, especially during the winter months when there are few holidaymakers about, Plymouth Laira-allocated Class 121 'bubblecar' No W55020 awaits departure time at Liskeard on 19 February 1982 as the 18.25 train for Looe.

Class 121 powercar No W55022, and attendant driving trailer, pass near King's Sutton on 8 May 1982, forming the 12.20 Oxfordshire stopping service from Oxford to Banbury, a 35min run along the Great Western 'Birmingham Direct' line. The motor brake second seats 65, while the driving trailer now has provision for 91, four seats having been lost when a corridor connection was fitted to the 'dumb' end. This was done to allow the vehicles to be used with other types of DMU as driving trailers, should the need arise to replace a driving car from another unit while repairs were carried out.

With Reading depot being unable to allocate a trailer vehicle for the service, two 'bubblecars' were run together as the 15.02 Reading-Bedwyn train on 14 June 1985. No W55030 leads No W55031 near Southcote Junction, Reading.

Replacing the usual Class 117 powercar, Class 121 No 55020 leads the remaining two vehicles of Reading set No L409 on the 10.34 Paddington-Reading local service. The single unit railcar has been painted into brown and cream at Swindon works as part of the 'GWR 150' celebrations and is passing Waltham St Lawrence, near Twyford, on 16 February 1987. *Colin J. Marsden*

Painted from brown and cream into the red, white, blue and grey of Network SouthEast (NSE), 'bubblecar' No 55020 arrives at King's Sutton station on 10 September 1987, forming the 17.12 local service from Banbury to Oxford. *John C. Baker*

The three-plus-two high-density seating arrangement of a Pressed Steel Class 121 interior, re-upholstered with the blue moquette of NSE.

In 1986, services operated by the West Midlands Passenger Transport Executive were given the brand name 'MidLine', and Tyseley-allocated 'bubblecar' No 55033 was provided with a new livery of two-tone blue with a red band. Later the red was also painted blue, giving the vehicle paintwork in three shades of the same colour. As Tyseley unit No T133 (originally numbered 083), it approaches Stourbridge Junction on 28 November 1987, working the shuttle on the three-quarter-mile branch from Stourbridge Town.

At the terminus end of the shortest passenger branch line in the UK, No 55033 shows its livery and 'MidLine' branding at Stourbridge Town on the same day.

A pair of Pressed Steel Class 121 'bubblecars', No 55022 and No 55025, scurry past Southall on 4 February 1990, as an empty stock movement from Old Oak Common depot to one or other of the London area branch lines. Two styles of NSE livery are apparent here: the leading car has the body stripes turned upwards at the cab ends, whereas the revised style has the stripes running straight across the bodywork.

Super bubble! No fewer than four Class 121 single unit railcars plus one Class 117 trailer form the 07.51 local service from Slough, arriving at Paddington on 13 April 1992. No 55025 leads vehicles Nos 55027, 55029, 59498 and 55024.

The last example of the Pressed Steel Class 121s to receive a full works overhaul and repaint was No 55023 at BRML Doncaster works in 1994, and the opportunity was taken to return it to original green livery with a half-yellow front panel. On 19 March 1994, it trundles along between Kempston Hardwick and Bedford Midland, working the 15.30 train from Bletchley to Bedford. The unit is displaying 'Cambridge' on the leading destination blind, and 'Oxford' on the rear one! It also now sports a centre headlight.

Operating as 'Sandite' units, ex-Class 121 'bubblecars' No 55030 and 55022 display their Departmental numbers 977866 (unit No 960013) and 977873, departing from Salisbury on 22 September 1995. They are passing Class 159 'South Western Turbo' No 159001. *Ken Brunt*

Some problems of rail privatisation have even affected the now venerable Class 121 'bubblecars'. To operate its non-electrified branch line, the FirstGroup plc-owned Great Eastern Railway (GER) used a Class 153 single-car unit sub-leased from Anglia Railways. Then, Anglia Railways found that it needed the unit itself and in September 1997, 'asked for its train back'. As a company operating only electric motive power, GER had nothing with which to operate the line. As a result, three stored Class 121s from North London Railways (now Silverlink Train Services) were brought back into traffic and used by GER on sub-lease until a second generation Class 153 'bubblecar' could be returned during the summer timetable 1998. On 29 September 1997, No 55031 arrives at Chappel & Wakes Colne as the 15.40 train from Sudbury to Marks Tey, and passes the East Anglian Railway Museum's preserved Class 108 DMCL cars No 52053 and No 51568.

Great Eastern branding and a Marks Tey-Sudbury logo on No 55031 at Marks Tey on the same day.

Gloucester RC&W Single Unit Railcar Class 122/131

Built by:	Gloucester Railway Carriage & Wagon Company
Introduced:	May 1958
Coupling Code:	Blue Square ■
Engines in each Driving Motor:	Two BUT (AEC) six-cylinder horizontal type 150hp
Transmission:	Mechanical, Standard
Body:	64ft 6in x 9ft 3in
Weight:	DMBS 35 tons
	DTS 29 tons
Operating numbers:	DMBS 55000 to 55019
	DTS 56291 to 56299

The fleet of 20 Gloucester RC&W single unit railcars was constructed at the same time as the Gloucester cross-country units, later to become Class 119. As a result, the two types shared many details, but the single units had a driving cab at either end and were built without gangways and with side doors to each seating bay. This was in accordance with the BR Derby high-density suburban layout at the time for branch line and local services. Like the later Class 121 vehicles, they could be used to augment other 'blue square' DMUs, in addition to operating as required with any of the nine single unit driving trailers built by the Gloucester works at the same time. Initially allocated to Western Region, and working both in London and in the Midlands, some found their way to Scotland. Line closures, however, restricted usefulness, and the majority were converted for parcels or Departmental operation, the last being withdrawn from passenger traffic in 1994. In 1968, three units, Nos Sc55013, 55014 and 55015, had all passenger seating removed and the entrance doors converted for double access, and were reclassified 131 for use as parcels vehicles. After transfer for Departmental service, however, they reverted again to Class 122. Two Gloucester '122s' are still in service for English Welsh & Scottish Railway and Railtrack, respectively, No 55012 being used as an inspection saloon and route learning vehicle, and ex-No 55019 becoming a 'Sandite' application unit. A total of six are in preservation, and can currently be seen on the Battlefield Line and on the Mid-Norfolk, Northampton & Lamport, and South Devon Railways. Class number 122 was given to the powercars, and the driving trailers became Class 150. None of the latter have survived, however, the last being scrapped in late 1982.

Gloucester RC&W single unit railcar No W55004 departs from Birmingham Snow Hill station on 21 March 1960, forming a local service for Dudley. Finished in malachite green with yellow lining, white cab roof canopies and 'speed whiskers', the vehicles that were to constitute Class 122 also had a two-panel route indicator below the centre cab window and exhaust stacks at one end, joined at the top with a single outlet. These are of a different design to the Class 121s, as they did not have to branch out at roof level to accommodate a headcode box. *R. C. Riley*

With a driving trailer attached, Gloucester single-railcar No W55006 emerges from Southall depot on 16 July 1960 to gain the Great Western main line with a special working, probably for driver familiarisation. In the left background are two GWR/AEC railcars, and on the right can be seen a variety of steam motive power in addition to a Gloucester parcels car. Because of the route indicator panels below the front cab windows, the 'speed whiskers' are unable to join at the 'V'. *C. R. Lewis Coles*

An excellent Gloucester RC&W single car profile, clearly showing the nine doors. The one at each end accesses the driving cab, one is for the guard, and six are for passengers to gain entry to the 65 second class seats provided. On 8 June 1963, vehicle No W55005 passes near Eardington, forming the 20.00 Bridgnorth to Kidderminster 'Severn Valley' line service. *Michael Mensing*

Gloucester RC&W single unit railcar No W55008 leaves the Bicester line at Aynho Junction on 29 August 1962, forming the 16.02 local service from Princes Risborough to Banbury. Although other cars still retained original 'speed whiskers', this example has already received a half-yellow front-end warning panel. *Michael Mensing*

The Gloucester RC&W single unit railcar interior, showing the original moquette and leatherette seats arranged three by two. Interior finish was plastic bonded onto hardboard, with a 'Laconite' ceiling. *Ian Allan Library*

BR Swindon Inter-City three- or four-car Class 123

Built by:	British Rail Swindon Works
Introduced:	February 1963
Coupling Code:	Blue Square ■
Engines in each Driving Motor:	Two BUT (Leyland Albion) six-cylinder horizontal type 230hp
Transmission:	Mechanical, Standard
Body:	64ft 11⅛in x 9ft 3in
Weight:	DMBSL 41 tons 14cwt
	DMSK 41 tons 9cwt
	TSL 31 tons 9cwt
	TCKL 32 tons 3cwt
	TSLRB 32 tons
Operating numbers:	DMBSL 52086 to 52095
	DMSK 52096 to 52105
	TSL 59235 to 59239
	TCKL 59818 to 59827
	TSLRB 59828 to 59832

Built at Swindon works between February and June 1963, to a new 'Inter-City' design (the nomenclature 'InterCity' came much later), the vehicles as new consisted of 10 of each type of powercar, 10 trailer composites, five trailer seconds and five trailer seconds with a buffet. Pullman-type gangway connections were fitted to both ends of all vehicles, allowing passengers access to any part of the train whatever the number of coaches in use. The driving cabs were designed to the side of the gangway connection, and passenger accommodation was at least the equivalent of the best locomotive-hauled stock of the day. Originally all cars were equipped with two lavatories, except the buffet trailers, which had one small lavatory for staff use only. The trains were first based at Cardiff to operate Swansea-Birmingham-Derby services, with a few turns to Plymouth, but after only two years they were transferred to the Cardiff-Bristol-Portsmouth turns. They did not last very long here either, and were transferred to Reading depot for use on Paddington-Oxford 'outer suburban' duties, followed by a short spell at Cardiff again on Cardiff-Crewe workings. The buffet trailers were short-lived, and all were withdrawn in September 1970, one being transferred to Departmental stock as a messing coach at Old Oak Common depot, and another, No W59831, converted to trailer vehicle No 69108 of Class 309 EMU No 309616. Classifications for the cars prior to being grouped together as Class 123 were:

123/1	Driving Motor Second with side corridor
123/2	Driving Motor Brake Second with lavatory
182	Trailer Second with lavatory
183	Trailer Composite with side corridor
184	Trailer Second with Buffet and staff lavatory

After a form of rolling stock rationalisation in 1977, units with similar engines were grouped together for maintenance purposes, and the Swindon Inter-City sets, most of which were now in store at Barry, found themselves transferred to Eastern Region at Botanic Gardens depot, Hull, where the Leyland Albion-engined Class 124 'Trans-Pennine' units were allocated. The two types then commenced working together, and a variety of combinations became possible, with some four-car sets consisting of '123' powercars with '124' trailers, and vice versa, and other units powered by driving motors from both types. Also, 10 Class 124 'Trans-Pennine' motor brakes were converted to trailers by having their power equipment removed, and were grouped with Class 123. These lasted in service until May 1984, and are more fully detailed under Class 124. Neither the Class 123 nor 124 stock was included in the BR refurbishment scheme and they were displaced on 'Trans-Pennine' diagrams by locomotive-hauled trains. All had been withdrawn by summer 1984, and most were cut up at Snailwell by breakers, Mayer Newman. None survive in preservation.

Introduced just four months previously, BR Swindon DMSL No W52096 leads four and three-car 'Inter-City' formations, passing Kings Norton on 3 June 1963 and forming a service from Cardiff to Birmingham and Derby. The livery is dark Brunswick green with cream lining and a white cab roof canopy. The front gangway connection has a yellow moulded plastic cover fitted, to hide the connecting door and protect the driver from draughts, and the four-character route indicator is split into two halves on either side.
Peter J. Shoesmith

Carrying a headboard reading 'Gilks-Greenside Educational Special No 6', a three-car Swindon 1963 'Inter-City' unit in blue and grey traverses Southern third-rail territory. Commencing from Clapham Junction, the special passes under the London Transport District Line bridge at Putney on 27 September 1969, heading for the National Tramway Museum at Crich, via Derby. The gangway cover is now black, and hinged with a centre opening. Ill-fitting at the base, it already looks draughty for the driver! *Brian Stephenson*

From the point of view of the passengers, the Swindon 1963-built 'Inter-City' units were the best of all the first generation stock, many lessons having been learnt over the previous decade. The new standard B4 and B5-type bogies beneath the trailers and powercars respectively, gave a particularly good ride at all speeds, and the seating layout with some corridor connected compartments was popular, providing good insulation against both noise and draughts. The driving cabs were slightly wrapped-round for good visibility, and they were fitted with buckeye couplers, as can clearly be seen here. On 16 May 1973, Class 123/1 DMBSL No W52101 leads set No L706 departing from Paddington as an evening service for Reading and Oxford. Unlike most of the class, the grey paintwork around the windows has stopped short and does not extend to cover the driver's door.

Passing Class 50 No 50026, the 18.18 Paddington-Didcot train departs from the London terminus on 21 May 1975, and passes under Ranelagh Bridge. Class 123/1 DMBS No W52096 of set No L715 leads two three-car formations. The fitted cover over the gangway connection is embossed 'BR' on each side of the centre opening.

The Class 123 BR Swindon 'Inter-City' units commenced a new lease of life when between June 1977 and May 1979 they were transferred to Botanic Gardens depot, Hull, to work a revamped Trans-Pennine timetable alongside the similar Leyland Albion-engined Class 124 units. The majority were sent to Swindon works for refurbishment prior to taking on their new role, but some were attended to at Lincoln depot, where unit No L711 is seen with new-style marker light boxes. Consisting of DMBSL No W52094, TCL No W59823 and DMSL No W52091, the unit is standing on the former Great Northern Railway 'Fens Line' at Lincoln, now in use as sidings for the depot. *Rev Graham Wise*

Class 123/2 motor brake No E52095 under maintenance inside Botanic Gardens depot on 31 August 1980.

With line maintenance taking place on the Hope Valley route, a Sunday Manchester-Sheffield train is diverted via Woodhead on 10 February 1980. Passing Torside, a mixed Class 123/124 set has 'Inter-City' motor brake No E52095 facing the camera. The now redundant four-character route indicator panels have been replaced by white-on-black marker lights, and the gangway connection no longer has a cover. *Les Nixon*

A profile of Class 183 Trailer Composite No E59825 at Botanic Gardens depot on 31 August 1980. These vehicles contained 24 seats for first class and the same number for standard class, and had two lavatories. The ventilated windows for these show at each end of the vehicle.

The disparate front end designs of 1963-built Class 123 and 1960-built Class 124 units inside Hull station on 31 August 1980. '123/2' DMS No E52092 displays odd-painted marker light surrounds, one yellow and one black. The units lead the 11.08 service to Sheffield and the 12.15 to Leeds, respectively.

The 10.11 train from Hull arrives at its Doncaster destination on 21 January 1981, formed of three Swindon 'Inter-City' vehicles and a Swindon 'Trans-Pennine' trailer. Class 123/1 powercar No E52015 leads Class 183 trailer composite No E59819, Class 180 'Trans-Pennine' trailer second No E59765 and Class 123/2 motor brake No E52094.

Class 123 motor brakes seated 32 in second class, whereas the motor seconds could accommodate 56. To recoup seating capacity lost by having two motor brakes in one unit, the 17 four-car sets made up by mixing the remaining Class 123 and 124 vehicles were re-formed again from 1981, to keep the individual powercar types together. At the same time the trailer composite vehicles were downgraded to second class only. With motor brake No E52089 leading, the 09.33 Leeds to Morecambe train passes Settle Junction on 8 February 1983. The four-character headcode box has been removed and replaced by marker lights.

BR Swindon 'Trans-Pennine' six-car Class 124

Built by:	British Rail Swindon Works	
Introduced:	July 1960	
Coupling Code:	Blue Square ∎	
Engines in each Driving Motor:	Two BUT (Leyland Albion) 6cyl horizontal type 230hp	
Transmission:	Mechanical, Standard	
Body:	64ft 6in x 9ft 3in	
Weight:	DMC	40 tons
	MBSK	41 tons
	TSL	32 tons
	TBFL	34 tons
Operating numbers:	DMC	51951 to 51967
	MBSK	51968 to 51984
	TSL	59765 to 59773
	TBFL	59774 to 59781
Renumbered:	51969 to 59834, 51978 to 59836, 51973 to 59841,	
	51980 to 59842, 51974 to 59835, 51981 to 59833,	
	51975 to 59839, 51983 to 59840, 51976 to 59838,	
	51984 to 59837	

Constructed at BR Swindon works for the North Eastern Region, these six-car trains were immediately recognisable, having what was then considered as modern-looking wrap-around driving cab windows, the BR Design Panel having been involved. In all, 51 vehicles were delivered during 1960 to Neville Hill depot, Leeds, and consisted of 17 driving motor composites, 17 motor brake seconds, nine trailer seconds and eight buffet firsts. From this fleet, eight six-car sets were formed, leaving one vehicle of each type as spare. When numerical classification was required for the BR TOPS computer, the four types became:

124/1	Driving Motor Composite
124/2	Motor Brake Second with side corridor (non-driving)
180	Trailer Standard with lavatory
181	Trailer Buffet First with lavatory

With two powered trailers in each consist, besides the usual driving motors, each unit had four powered vehicles, providing an impressive 1,840hp with which to tackle the demanding Trans-Pennine route, via Standedge and Diggle. After Botanic Gardens depot, Hull, had been re-equipped, the 'Trans-Pennine' units were transferred in from Neville Hill and continued to work from the Hull depot until their final demise, along with the Class 123 Swindon 'Inter-City' units, in 1984. The coming of the M62 motorway resulted in a decline in passenger numbers between Yorkshire and Lancashire, and the first casualties were the eight Class 181 buffet cars, withdrawn from 1972. The five-car units soldiered on, joined by the Class 123s and shuffled in with them to form 17 four-car mixed sets. Now having a sufficient number of driving motors, 10 Class 124/2 non-driving motor brakes were converted to trailer vehicles by having the power equipment removed, and were renumbered as detailed above. To combat road transport, locomotive-hauled stock was introduced on the Trans-Pennine route, and the last Swindon Class 124 was withdrawn with the 1963 'Inter-City' sets in the summer of 1984. Like the '123s', no example of this interesting type has been preserved.

In cream-lined Brunswick green, and without either 'speed whiskers' or yellow warning panel, Driving Motor Composite No E51964 leads a six-car BR Swindon 'Trans-Pennine' unit passing near Birstall on 8 March 1961. The four-character route indicator panel, a last-minute addition to the design, shows '1N99', indicating that this was a Leeds-Huddersfield service. Observe the two coach nameboards at cant-rail level on intermediate vehicles. *Gavin Morrison*

In addition to 18 first class seats, the 'Trans-Pennine' buffet trailers provided for eight chairs at two tables. Initially, the 'Griddle', as it was called, was very popular with passengers, and provided refreshments levelled midway between the usual tea and sandwiches and a full meal service. The best-selling items were a hot Angus steak in a toasted bread roll, and bangers and mash. *Ian Allan Library*

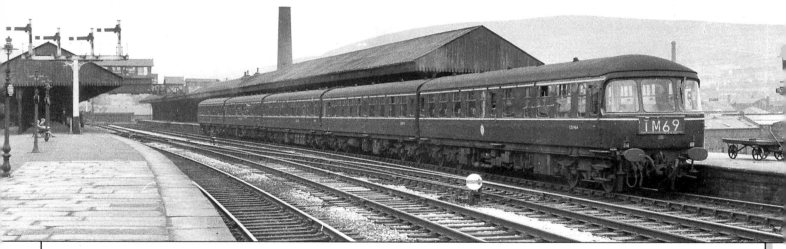

With one of the two powered trailers missing, a five-car 'Trans-Pennine' set departs from a forlorn-looking Stalybridge station on 27 July 1962. Driving motor No E51964 leads the 13.35 train from Hull to Liverpool Lime Street. *John N. Faulkner*

Approaching Milnsbridge, near Huddersfield, on 9 July 1966, a Trans-Pennine service from Hull to Liverpool Lime Street is led by driving motor No E51963. A half-yellow front warning panel is now in evidence, together with a light grey roof, and again the usual six-car set has been reduced to five. On this occasion it is the trailer second that is missing from the formation, meaning that four of the five vehicles are powered! *Gavin Morrison*

On 30 March 1967, the 15.45 Leeds-Liverpool Lime Street service crosses Saddleworth viaduct, formed of a six-car Swindon 'Trans-Pennine' set, with driving motor No E51952 leading. Not being suburban units, these sets were not painted into BR all-over blue, but went straight from original green livery to blue and grey. The rear powercar has already been so treated. *John Clarke*

With fewer diagrams on Sundays, the 'Trans-Pennine' DMUs were very popular for 'rest day' excursions, particularly in their early days with the buffet facility being open throughout. With passengers heading for trips on the Talyllyn and Welshpool & Llanfair Railways, DMC No E51955 leads a full six-car set on arrival at Welshpool from Bradford Exchange, on 11 June 1967. *Stanley Creer*

With the buffet now removed, a standard five-car 'Trans-Pennine' set in blue/grey livery with a full-yellow front end emerges from Morley tunnel, south of Leeds, on 2 March 1972. Forming a Hull to Liverpool Lime Street train, driving motor No E51963 leads. These composite vehicles seated 21 in first class immediately behind the driver, and 36 in second. The seats were arranged in a two-plus-one configuration in 'first' and two-plus-two in 'second', instead of the usual three-plus-two in most other DMUs. Both first and second class sections had window curtains. *John Cooper-Smith*

With Class 124/1 driving motor composite No E51954 facing the camera, a Manchester-bound 'Trans-Pennine' unit makes the scheduled stop at Selby on 14 June 1977. Passing on the centre road, a northbound train of coal hoppers is powered by Class 37s, No 37085 leading No 37216.

The Class 124/2 non-driving powercars were delivered already wired up for easy conversion to driving units if required, but the facility was never taken up. The 48 second class seats in them were arranged in similar style to Mk1 locomotive-hauled corridor coaching stock, with six four-a-side compartments. In 1981, 10 of the remaining vehicles had their traction equipment removed and were reclassified as trailer brake seconds, being renumbered accordingly. With power equipment intact, motor brake No E51976 stands at Leeds on 2 July 1977. This vehicle became trailer brake No E59838. *Michael Mensing*

Another view of Selby station before it lost its main line and major junction status in 1983. Now fitted with white discs illuminated from the rear, in place of route indicator blinds, DMCL No E51967 leads a train for Hull on 13 January 1979. Only three vehicles of 'Trans-Pennine' stock are being utilised, the rear powercar being a Metro-Cammell Class 111. *Rex Kennedy*

Operating as standard DMUs, with two driving cars and two trailers, the Class 124 units were introduced on Manchester-South Humberside services in 1979. With powercar No E51963 leading, the 12.45 from Manchester Piccadilly to Cleethorpes leaves Doncaster on 11 April 1980. *John E. Oxley*

Still having to carry a rear tail lamp, a four-car Class 124 unit makes the scheduled Scunthorpe stop on 1 September 1980, forming the 08.45 service from Manchester Piccadilly to Cleethorpes. Driving motor No E51952 is facing the camera. The hooks originally provided for coachboards are still in evidence.

Having just passed a main line steam special travelling in the opposite direction, the 12.00 Leeds-Morecambe train passes near Hellifield on 5 February 1983, the four-car Class 124 unit led by driving motor No E51963. The black surround to the marker light box has been painted yellow, and marker lights have been inserted in place of the previous illuminated white discs.

Although Hull Botanic Gardens depot carried out routine maintenance on the Class 124 fleet, major overhauls took place at Doncaster works. With four digits of the vehicle number shown between the marker lights, driving motor No E51951 receives attention in the DMU shop on 12 September 1981.
Colin J. Marsden

Rostered for the 12.39 Morecambe-Leeds train, a four-car Class 124 'Trans-Pennine' unit passes near Wennington on 8 February 1983.

The original six-car 'Trans-Pennine' sets contained two driving motors, two motor brakes, a trailer and a trailer buffet. This six-car formation on 10 December 1983 consists of three driving motors and three trailers, the fourth and sixth cars being powered besides the leading vehicle. The 12.45 Manchester Piccadilly-Cleethorpes service is passing Brightside, near Sheffield.

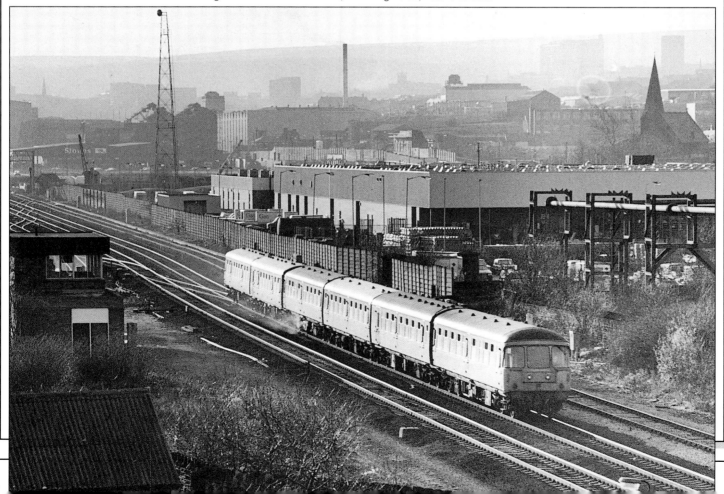

BR Derby/Rolls-Royce three-car Class 125

Built by:	British Rail Derby Works
Introduced:	December 1958
Coupling Code:	Orange Star ✳
Engines in each Driving Motor:	Two Rolls-Royce eight-cylinder horizontal type 238hp
Transmission:	Hydraulic. Twin-disc torque converter
Body:	64ft 0in x 9ft 3in
Weight:	DMS 39 tons 10cwt
	DMBS 39 tons 10cwt
	TS 28 tons 10cwt
Operating numbers:	DMS 50988 to 51007
	DMBS 51154 to 51173
	TS 59449 to 59468

A total of 20 three-car high-density suburban units were built at BR Derby works between December 1958 and September 1959 for Eastern Region's Lea Valley services between London Liverpool Street and Broxbourne. Powered by eight-cylinder Rolls-Royce engines of 238hp, the units were non-standard, but the extra power was needed for the climb out of Liverpool Street to Bethnal Green, particularly during weekday evening peak hours when the trains would be heavily laden. Unfortunately, they proved unreliable in traffic, the hydraulic transmission being a particular weakness, in the same way as with the Rolls-Royce-engined Cravens units, described under Class 113. Displaced from the Lea Valley route after electrification, the units were found work elsewhere on Eastern Region, particularly on suburban

services out of King's Cross, where the climb away from the terminus was probably even more demanding than from Liverpool Street. Their continued unreliability, however, as well as the operational disadvantage of the 'Orange Star' coupling code, resulted in a decision being taken to withdraw the complete fleet. All were taken out of traffic by January 1977, except for two trailers that continued in Departmental use. These too were finally broken up in 1986 and 1988, respectively. None of the fleet has been preserved, although they did survive long enough to receive TOPS classifications as follows:

125/1	Driving Motor Second
125/2	Driving Motor Brake Second
185	Trailer Second

Posed in the snow of January 1959 for official photographs, a brand-new three-car BR Derby/Rolls-Royce unit displays the standard 'Derby'-style front end of the period. Consisting of driving motor second No E50993, trailer second No E59454 and driving motor brake second No E51159, the set is finished in unlined Brunswick green livery, with white cab roof canopy, two-character headcode panel, two marker lights and yellow 'speed whiskers'. In the same way as other high-density units from Derby, bodyside doors are provided to each seating bay throughout the train, there are no toilet facilities, and no gangway connections between the three vehicles. *Ian Allan Library*

Having been in service for only eight months, a BR Derby/Rolls-Royce unit arrives at Braintree on 12 September 1959, forming the 17.59 train from Witham. The set consists of DMS No E51005, TS No E59466 and DMBS No E51171. The trailer became the longest surviving car in the whole Class 125 fleet. It was taken into Departmental use as a fire test vehicle in December 1976, and was finally broken up at Vic Berry of Leicester in July 1988. *John N. Faulkner*

The 10.47 Saturday service from London Liverpool Street to Harwich Town passes Stratford on 13 July 1963, formed of BR Derby/Rolls-Royce vehicles Nos E51156, E59451 and E50990, the former now having two yellow warning panels in place of the original 'speed whiskers'. Without toilet facilities or inter-carriage gangway connections, travelling on this train was unlikely to have been very pleasant for anyone making the complete journey of over 70 miles! *John N. Faulkner*

While working Lea Valley services, the Derby/Rolls-Royce units were allocated to Stratford Depot, in east London. Seen there on 15 December 1968, driving motor brake No E51154 displays a complete half-yellow front-end warning panel. *David Percival*

Now displaced from Lea Valley services following upon electrification of the route, the 15.00 train from Hatfield North to King's Cross is formed of a Derby/Rolls-Royce three-car DMU. The date is 2 August 1969 and the location at Harringay West is typical of the Great Northern route around London at this time. *John N. Faulkner*

The BR Derby/Rolls-Royce units arrived on the ex-Great Northern line in May 1959 and were used mainly on inner suburban services, gaining a few outer suburban diagrams later. On a drab-looking day in November 1972, two BR Derby Class 125 units await departure from the King's Cross suburban platforms. Driving motor brakes Nos E51154 and E51165 head trains for Hertford North and Welwyn Garden City, respectively, and both now wear all-over BR 'corporate blue' livery with full-yellow ends. *Brian Beer*

Carrying a tail lamp, a four-car Cravens Class 105 DMU heads southbound away from the camera towards Enfield Chase on 12 September 1973, and passes a six-car formation of Derby/Rolls-Royce Class 125 units approaching Gordon Hill, on the Hertford Loop. The Cravens set heads for King's Cross, while the Rolls-Royce-engined trains are for Hertford North. *Ken Brunt*

In April snow, two Class 125 three-car units form the 07.10 Sandy-King's Cross train and approach Stevenage on 9 April 1975. *David Percival*

With Class 125/2 motor brake No E51161 leading, a three-car Rolls-Royce-engined Derby unit heads south from Potters Bar on 6 December 1975, forming the 10.04 service from Stevenage to King's Cross. The two-character headcode panel is now redundant, and the unit itself will soon come under the same category, as overhead wires are in position for the King's Cross inner suburban services to be energised in the following year.

Climbing away from Potters Bar tunnel on the same day, a Class 125 unit forms the 11.40 local stopping service from King's Cross to Welwyn Garden City, an overall journey time of 47min. Allowing for the upgrade of the East Coast main line, and the fact that electric multiple units now operate the service, the reduction in time for the same journey today is about 10 minutes.

Prior to being finally withdrawn on the first day of 1977, the Class 125 Derby/Rolls-Royce units remaining in service were placed into store during the preceding three months, mostly at Finsbury Park and Stratford. Various breakers' torches soon beckoned, however, and they were dispersed around the country to Booth Roe Metals of Rotherham, the Bird Group at Long Marston, and to both Derby and Doncaster works. At Doncaster 'Plant' on 10 August 1980, driving motor second No E50991 has the doors removed and awaits final disposal.

BR Swindon 'Inter-City' three and six-car Class 126

Built by:	British Rail Swindon Works
Introduced:	May 1959
Coupling Code:	White Circle ●
Engines in each Driving Motor:	Two BUT (AEC) six-cylinder horizontal type 150hp
Transmission:	Mechanical, Standard
Body:	64ft 6in x 9ft 3in
Weight:	DMSL 38 tons
	DMBSL 38 tons
	TFK 32 tons
	TCL 30 tons
	TBFKL 33 tons
Operating numbers:	DMSL 50936 and 51008 to 51029
	DMBSL 51030 to 51051
	TFK 59391 to 59400
	TCL 59402 to 59412
	TBFKL 59098 to 59099

The second order to Swindon works for 'Inter-City' units for Scottish Region was basically the same as the 1956-7 batch described under 'First Orders'. The vehicles retained the arrangement of two different front ends that enabled three-car units to be coupled in a six-car formation and retain gangway access from one set to the other. They also had the same 'white circle' coupling code as the earlier units, to allow the two types to work together in multiple. A total of 45 powercars was produced, allied to 23 trailer vehicles of three different types, 10 corridor firsts, 11 composites and two buffet firsts, all later declassified to second class only as TSLs. The rise of passenger numbers on the Edinburgh-Glasgow route outgrew the capacity of 'Inter-City' DMUs, and they were replaced first by pairs of Class 27 locomotives working on a push-pull basis with Mk2 coaching stock, and later with Mk 3 stock powered by Class 47/7s with driving brakes on one end, converted from Mk2f BSOs. The remaining BR Swindon 'Inter-City' units were concentrated on the Ayrshire services. They remained there until supplanted by Class

101 and 107 units, which had a standard 'Blue Square' coupling code, and did not cause the same operating frustrations. The two trailer buffet first vehicles were withdrawn from traffic prior to commencement of numerical classifications. TOPS numbers for the other types of vehicle, prior to them being grouped together as Class 126 were:

126/1	Driving Motor Second with lavatory
126/2	Driving Motor Brake Second with lavatory
187	Trailer Buffet First with lavatory
189	Trailer First with side corridor
	Trailer Composite with lavatory

A three-car Class 126 set, comprising vehicles Sc51017, Sc59404 and Sc51043, has been preserved on the Bo'ness & Kinneil Railway. The two buffet trailers withdrawn in October 1972 survived for another 22 years as camping coaches on the North Yorkshire Moors Railway, but were eventually broken up by MC Metal Processing of Glasgow in May 1994.

Formed of driving motor No Sc51023, trailer composite No Sc59402 and driving motor brake No Sc51034, a three-car 1959-built BR Swindon 'Inter-City' unit arrives at Kilmarnock from Glasgow Central on 20 May 1960, seven months after introduction. The fleet were painted in Brunswick green livery, with cream lining, and the 'intermediate' driving motors were fitted with a two-character headcode panel on each side of the gangway connection. This left no room for the usual 'speed whiskers' which, nevertheless, were still displayed on the 'leading' end of each unit, as shown in the following illustration. *John N. Faulkner*

In the same way as the 1956 Swindon 'Inter-City' build, these later units had two distinctly different driving ends. This example of 'leading' motor brake No Sc51032 shows the usual Swindon-style driving window arrangement, below which are two closely grouped two-panel headcode boxes. The vehicles were not provided with either marker lights or destination blinds. The location is Largs, and the six-car train has arrived as the 13.47 from Glasgow St Enoch, on 19 May 1960. *John N. Faulkner*

Despite being classified 'Inter-City', the Class 126 units were at first repainted into BR overall-blue instead of blue and grey, as they were not diagrammed for express running on the Ayrshire lines. With each side of the 'intermediate' end painted yellow, but the gangway connection still in black, DMS No Sc51024 leads the three-car 15.00 Glasgow Central-Stranraer train on 9 August 1972. The yellow line at cant-rail level on the trailer composite vehicle shows the position of the 18 first class seats, the remaining 32 being standard class. The location is south of New Luce station, which closed in 1965. *Michael Mensing*

Braking for the stop at Prestwick, a three-car Class 126 unit displays headcode '2A27', indicating that this is the 12.35 service from Glasgow Central to Ayr. Driving motor standard 'intermediate' No Sc51015 is leading, and has provision for 64 seats.

Passing the old Glasgow & South Western Railway signalbox at the northern approach to Ayr, the same train arrives at its destination on 2 June 1977. Like other Swindon-built corridor vehicles, the gangway cover of DMS No Sc51015 is embossed 'BR'.

Headed by 'intermediate' Class 126/1 powercar No Sc51020, a six-car Class 126 unit awaits departure from Ayr on 2 June 1977, forming the 16.45 train to Glasgow Central. The faithful oil lamp from the incoming working will be removed before the train leaves. In the through platforms is a BR Derby Class 107 unit, one of the types that replaced the '126s' on these services after they were withdrawn as non-standard in 1981-2.

The 13.36 train from Stranraer to Glasgow Central restarts from the Ayr stop on the same day. The six-car BR Swindon 'Inter-City' formation is headed by 'leading' Class 126/2 motor brake No Sc51035 which seats 52 in standard class accommodation. At this time, Scottish Region DMUs began to receive unit numbers, this one being 415, as shown beneath the driver's front window.

Sharing Ayr depot with a variety of Classes 08, 20, 26 and 47 diesel locomotives, Class 126/1 DMSL No Sc51013 emerges to form a service for Glasgow Central on 3 June 1977.

Without proper marker lights being installed, the Class 126 units were always obliged to carry tail lamps when in traffic. Now in blue and grey colours, and carrying a Greater Glasgow Passenger Transport Executive 'Trans-Clyde' logo, Class 126/2 'leading' motor brake No Sc51037 stands at the rear of an arrival at Carlisle from Ayr on 3 November 1979. The headcode panel has been blacked out, leaving two illuminated white dots. *Graham Scott-Lowe*

A front-end close-up of Class 126/1 'intermediate' powercar No Sc51024 on depot at Ayr on 30 March 1980. The gangway connection has been removed and the end plated over and the headcode boxes have marker dots on a black background. *Tom Noble*

Flanked by BR Swindon Class 126 units Nos 400 and 417, Class 47/4 No 47435 waits to leave Ayr with the 11.00 through service from Stranraer to London Euston, on 27 August 1980. The unit on the left still retains an original headcode panel at this stage. *Les Nixon*

With the gangway connection plated over and marker dots aglow, '126/1' driving motor No Sc51018 leads the 11.00 train from Glasgow Central to Ayr, at Johnstone on 26 January 1981.

A three-car Class 126 set on the 11.35 Glasgow Central to Stranraer service approaches Falkland yard, on the outskirts of Ayr, on 15 June 1981. Driving brake No Sc51039 leads trailer standard No Sc59406 and driving motor second No Sc51029. The set number 409 is now prefixed by the unit class number 126. The front-end route indicator still remains, and the train reporting number, 1A27, is just visible beneath the grime on the panels. *Rex Kennedy*

BR Derby/Rolls-Royce four-car Class 127

Built by:	British Rail Derby Works
Introduced:	May 1959
Coupling Code:	Red Triangle ▲
Engines in each Driving Motor:	Two Rolls-Royce eight-cylinder horizontal type 238hp
Transmission:	Hydraulic, Torque Converter
Body:	64ft 0in x 9ft 3ins

Weight:	DMBS	40 tons
	TSL	30 tons
	TS	29 tons

Operating numbers:	DMBS	51591 to 51650
	TSL	59589 to 59618
	TS	59619 to 59648

Renumbered:	51591 to 55966, 51619 to 55985, 51596 to 55982,
	51624 to 55983, 51597 to 55971, 51625 to 55976,
	51600 to 55979, 51627 to 55986, 51603 to 55977,
	51633 to 55980, 51606 to 55969, 51635 to 55970
	51608 to 55978, 51637 to 55968, 51610 to 55967,
	51639 to 55984, 51611 to 55972, 51640 to 55973,
	51612 to 55981, 51642 to 55974, 51615 to 55975,
	51649 to 55987

The British Rail Modernisation Plan of 1955 included electrification of the London St Pancras-Bedford route, but it was accorded a low priority. A stopgap fleet of dedicated DMUs was ordered to eliminate the steam-hauled non-corridor suburban stock then in use, and between May and December 1959, 60 driving motors and the same number of trailers emerged from Derby works to form 30 four-car trains. The more powerful Rolls-Royce eight-cylinder engine and torque converter was chosen for them, coupled to hydraulic transmission. This meant that the fleet was incompatible with most of the other new DMUs, but as they were not expected to operate away from the 'Bedpan' line outer-suburban services, it was considered not to matter. A 'red triangle' coupling code was employed for them, the same as used for 'Derby Lightweight' stock which had the Leyland 125hp engine and torque converter. Design of the fleet was obviously to the 'Derby' style of the period, and yet again corridors were omitted, despite the distance from London to Bedford being nearly 50 miles. Toilet facilities were provided in one trailer, but passengers in any of the other three vehicles in the unit could not reach them! Unlike most of the other Derby-designed high-density units, the fault was never remedied while they worked from St Pancras. Perhaps 'Bedpan' commuters were so used to not having such a 'luxury' that they did not complain. Alternatively, perhaps those travelling longer distances became aware of the situation, and used the appropriate coach — or was the total lack of any first class accommodation anything to do with it? Prior to the unit 127 classification, the powercars were designated 127, and all the trailers as 186.

The Rolls-Royce engines and hydraulic transmissions were always troublesome, and over the years the maintenance staff at Cricklewood depot were said to work minor miracles to keep services at an acceptable level. Electrification of the route finally started, and although the new Class 317 electric units for the services were initially 'blacked' by the driver's trade unions, the 22-year-old 'stopgap' Class 127s were finally withdrawn from the line in 1984. This was not the end of them, however, as 22 were converted for parcels and newspaper traffic, and lasted in service until 1989. Similarly, although the powercars were not included in the DMU refurbishment programme, some trailers were, and these also had an extended life in the West Midlands area. Coupled to a variety of other class types allocated to Tyseley depot, the last '186' was not finally withdrawn until October 1993! A total of eight powercars and two trailers are in preservation and can be seen on the Chacewater, Great Central, and South Devon Railways, and at the Midland Railway Centre and Rogart station, in the Scottish Highlands.

In June 1959, the third Rolls-Royce-engined four-car unit to emerge from BR Derby works is posed for an official photograph — although why the cameraman should have chosen a location where he was obliged to view it through telegraph wires is not apparent. However, the illustration depicts the original Brunswick dark green livery, with cream lining, 'speed whiskers', marker lights and a white cab roof canopy that houses four-character route indicator roller-blinds. The set consists of DMBS vehicles Nos M51594 and M51592, with TS No M59620 and TSL No M59590.
British Rail

Gloucester RC&W Single Unit Parcels Car Class 128

Built by:	Gloucester Railway Carriage & Wagon Company
Introduced:	January 1960
Coupling Code:	Blue Square ■
Engines in each Driving Motor:	Two BUT (Leyland Albion six-cylinder horizontal type 230hp
Transmission:	Mechanical, Standard
Body:	64ft 6in x 9ft 3in
Weight:	DMLV 40 tons or 41 tons
Operating numbers:	DMLV 55987 to 55996

The 10 driving motor luggage vans introduced from the Gloucester carriage works between January and April 1960 were initially allocated four to the London Midland Region and six to Western Region. The 'Western' cars had end gangways fitted but the 'Midland' batch did not. As a result, the LMR units, Nos M55987 to 55990, weighed one ton less. The design was purpose-built with good access, by way of three sets of double doors along the bodysides. With front-end gangway connections, the Western Region vehicles had the cab driving windows placed to one side in the manner of the BR Swindon 'Inter-City' units, and they were also similarly powered, with two Leyland Albion 230hp engines. Later redesignated as driving motor parcels and miscellaneous vans (DMPMV), the last LMR Class 128s were withdrawn from service in 1982, but five of the six WR vehicles lasted until late 1990, being cut up at MC Metal Processing, Glasgow, from April of the following year. None have been preserved.

Fresh from the manufacturers, the first of four Gloucester RC&W driving motor luggage vans for the London Midland Region, No M55987, is posed for an official camera in January 1960. The non-gangwayed 40ton vehicle is painted in green, lined out in yellow, and has a grey roof. The four-character route indicator panel, fitted below the front cab windows, is flanked by short individual 'speed whiskers' that make no attempt to join up, and it is fitted with squared-off buffer heads. Because of accident damage, this unit was withdrawn in July 1971 and subsequently scrapped at the yard of T.W. Ward of Beighton. *Colin J. Marsden collection*

The first Gloucester DMLV for Western Region, No W55991, heads towards Paddington, at Subway Junction, on 10 September 1960, operating a parcels shuttle from Slough. The 41ton vehicle is inscribed 'Parcels Service' in the same way as the 'Midland' vehicles, but has a roof of darker grey and a front-end gangway connection between the exhaust outlets. Small, somewhat cramped-looking 'speed whiskers' are painted onto the gangway connection cover, which has the four-character route indicator split on either side. The tail lamp is required, as marker lights were not a part of the original design specification. *R. C. Riley*

Operating the same 3A49 parcels service between Paddington and Slough on 1 April 1961, Gloucester car No W55996 passes West Ealing. With 460hp available from the two Leyland Albion engines fitted, the Gloucester cars could haul a sizeable vacuum-braked trailing load when required to do so. In this instance just two vehicles are in tow, a standard GUV and a 1940-vintage LNER-built bogie CCT. *Rodney Lissenden*

The first-built Gloucester RC&W DMLV car No M55987 now has its 'speed whiskers' obliterated by the application of a half-yellow warning panel. Compared with the first illustration in this section, the vehicle now has a dark grey roof and a warning label in the cab window about overhead electrification. *Ian Allan Library*

Looking rather dilapidated, in unlined blue with yellow end, Gloucester parcels car No M55990 stands in Buxton station on 4 September 1979, being loaded with mail. White marker light dots are now placed oddly in the outer panels of the redundant headcode panel. The vehicles have now been allocated class number 128.

A parcels service for Newtown, Powys, departs from Shrewsbury on 14 September 1981, formed of ex-Western Region parcels van No M55995. The gangway connection has been plated up, the headcode panel has been removed, marker lights are now fitted and the units are now designated as driving motor parcels and miscellaneous vans (DMPMV).

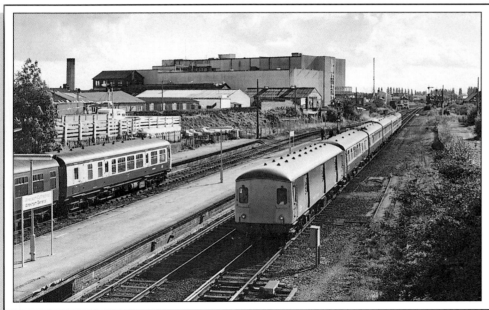

To avoid separate pathing, passenger and parcels services were sometimes amalgamated. Arriving at Wrexham General station on 18 September 1981, one such example shows ex-Western Region Class 128 No M55993 leading a three-car BR Swindon Class 120 unit and a Metro-Cammell Class 101 twin, to form the 13.48 working from Wolverhampton to Chester. All traces of the gangway connection have been removed, and a very bland front end now has just two cab windows and two fitted marker lights.

With a vacuum-fitted GUV in tow, Gloucester Class 128 DMPMV No M55994 forms a parcels train from Chester on 1 June 1984, entering Manchester Oxford Road station in unrelenting summer rain. This vehicle retains its split headcode boxes, with two marker dots inserted into the inner panels.

Two Gloucester '128s' allocated to Newton Heath in 1985-6 were repainted into 'Red Star' livery of two-tone blue with a centre red stripe, and the yellow front end was visually broken up by painting the section between the cab windows in black. Heading west onto the Cambrian line, 'Red Star'-liveried Class 128 No 55994 passes Sutton Bridge Junction, Shrewsbury, on 30 May 1986. No 55994 display a variation, with marker lights fitted into the old split headcode panels which are still evident despite the gangway connection having been removed and plated up. *John Tuffs*

The remaining Class 128 parcel vehicles allocated to Reading, and later Old Oak Common, had their gangway connections plated up, but remained in all-blue livery until the last examples received the 'Royal Mail' treatment in 1998. At Langley on 22 April 1987, the 13.40 parcels service from Reading to Paddington comprises No W55992. Rapidly overtaking is Class 47/4 No 47449, with the 11.40 Malago Vale-Old Oak Common vans train.

On 13 June 1987, the 13.20 mixed passenger/parcels train from Reading to Paddington passes West Drayton, driven from Class 128 vehicle No W55992. The passengers are seated in a Pressed Steel Company Class 117 three-car DMU, led by driving motor No W51397.

Painted into 'Royal Mail' colours of red with yellow markings and with the words 'Royal Mail Letters' on the bodysides, Class 128 No 55992 (the redundant 'W' prefix now omitted) passes Waltham St Lawrence on 9 July 1988. The DMPMV leads Class 121 No W55030 in blue/grey livery, and a three-car Class 117 unit in the red, white, blue and grey colours of Network SouthEast! The striking entourage forms the mixed 16.35 Reading-Paddington service. *Michael J. Collins*

With each vehicle powered by two 230hp Leyland Albion engines, two Class 128 units working in multiple provided one of the most powerful DMU formations available. Passing Wellingborough on 3 October 1988, Nos 55993 and 55994 form a northbound parcels service to Nottingham.

On 12 October 1990, the last run by a parcels DMU on British Rail occurred when Class 128 No 55993 arrived at London St Pancras, working from Chester, heading two Class 114/1 units and Class 128 No 55994, in lieu of the 'Irish Mail'. Once unloaded, the units formed the 20.40 empty stock working to Derby. Alongside, Class 43 powercar No 43121 is at the rear of the 20.00 High Speed Train service to Sheffield.

Cravens Single Unit Parcels Car Class 129

Built by:	Cravens Railway Carriage & Wagon Company (later Cravens Ltd)
Introduced:	July 1958
Coupling Code:	Yellow Diamond ◆
Engines in each Driving Motor:	Two BUT (AEC) six-cylinder horizontal type 150hp
Transmission:	Mechanical, Standard
Body:	57ft 6in x 9ft 3in
Weight:	DMLV 30 tons
Operating numbers:	DMLV 55997 to 55999

Cravens of Sheffield constructed three driving motor luggage vans (DMLVs) in July/August 1958 for use in the northwest of London Midland Region. Allocated to Newton Heath depot, they operated mainly in the Manchester area, with some journeys made south to Stafford and Wolverhampton and others north to Carlisle. Designed with driving cabs at both ends, but without gangway connections, they were capable of towing a trailing load and could couple with other 'yellow diamond'-coded 'Derby Lightweight' or first generation Metro-Cammell units. Three single standard slam-doors were fitted to each bodyside, and most of the side windows were backed with security iron bars. Classified 129, the three vehicles were withdrawn from traffic in 1972-3. No M55997, however, survived until 1986, working at Derby Research Centre as a hydraulic transmission testing vehicle. Provided with the title 'Laboratory No 9', it was named *Hydra*.

Cravens Driving Motor Luggage Van No M55998 stands at the end of Platforms 1 and 2 at Birmingham New Street station on 28 November 1958, a few months after entering service. In appearance, the front end of the vehicles closely resembled the Cravens passenger DMUs, being designed with the same two front cab windows and two-character headcode box. They were finished in dark green, with cream lining and 'speed whiskers', and were fitted with marker lamps. *Michael Mensing*

The front end of Cravens single unit parcels car No M55998, in ex-works condition in 1958. One 'whisker' crosses the small ventilation grille, and the 'Yellow Diamond' coupling code can clearly be seen. To avoid any possibility of error, the diamond is repeated on each of the four jumper lead receptacles, a practice not uncommon with non-'Blue Square' units. Only one windscreen wiper is fitted. *Colin J. Marsden collection*

On 4 March 1961, Cravens DMLV No M55999 backs along the southbound platform at Stafford, its parcels from Manchester having been unloaded. Although marker lamps were fitted, these were not of the later more-powerful type, and a rear oil lamp is in position. The attractive Stafford station roof has since been demolished. *Michael Mensing*

Cravens motor luggage van No M55998 is seen at Wolverhampton High Level station, awaiting a clear platform for loading. The two outer receptacles for the main jumper leads have been painted yellow, to ensure that any employee is aware that this is a 'Yellow Diamond' coded vehicle. Why the original yellow diamonds, as illustrated previously, were not sufficient for the purpose is unknown. The inner receptacles remain in the same green as the livery. *J. B. Bucknell*

With a trailing load of two vans, Cravens parcels car No M55998 stands in Platform 6 at Birmingham New Street station on 2 May 1964. It is still in green livery, but the 'whiskers' have now given way to a half-yellow front warning panel. *Michael Mensing*

On a very dull 9 September 1967, the mixed parcels/passenger 07.47 train from Whitehaven arrives at Carlisle. Behind the leading Cravens DMLV No M55997 is a two-car 'Derby Lightweight' unit, the first car of which is in original green livery, with the other being newly painted into plain blue. *John N. Faulkner*

In latter-day BR 'corporate blue', Cravens parcels car No M55999 stands at Stafford on 10 June 1969, having arrived from Manchester. As the 'Yellow Diamond' coupling code could not be seen on the all-yellow front end, the symbol has been given a black square surround. *John Glover*

A northbound parcels working awaits departure from Shrewsbury on 25 March 1972. The two Class 129 Cravens parcels units, Nos M55997 and M55999, are no longer designated as DMLVs, the new description being Driving Motor Parcels and Miscellaneous Vans (DMPMV). Attached to them is a 'Syphon G' van. *A. Wyn Hobson*

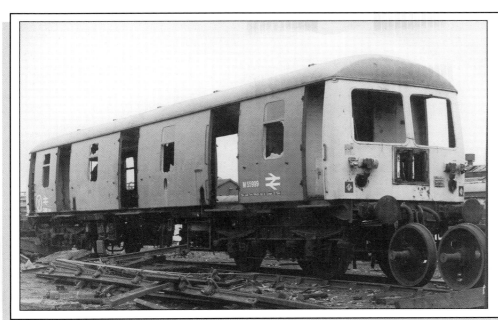

Looking justifiably sorry for itself, Class 129 car No M55999 is in the process of being scrapped at Derby Carriage & Wagon Works on 14 August 1976, having been moved there after withdrawal in October 1973.
R. I. Wallace

In the red and blue colours of the Derby Research Centre, ex-Cravens Class 129 No M55997 works the Old Dalby test track on 7 September 1980 as Departmental vehicle No DB975385 *Hydra*. In use at the time for a hydraulic traction development project, 'Laboratory 9' is operated by the power systems section at Derby, and has been fitted with modified B4 bogies. The vehicle was finally withdrawn and disposed of at the Leicester breaker's yard of Vic Berry in 1986.
Colin J. Marsden

THE SOUTHERN DEMUS
The 6xxxx series

BR Eastleigh six-car Class 201

Built by:	British Rail Eastleigh Works
Introduced:	January 1957
Coupling Code:	None, but within SR DEMU types only
Engines in each Driving Motor:	Two 500hp English Electric 4SRKT
Transmission:	Electrical. Two nose-suspended axle-hung traction motors
Body:	58ft 0in x 9ft 0in
Weight:	DMBS 54 tons 2cwt
	TSL 29 tons
	TFLK 30 tons
Operating numbers:	DMBS 60000 to 60013
	TSL 60500 to 60520
	TFLK 60700 to 60706

In February 1957, before the new Hastings diesels services were introduced in the summer of the same year, Class 6S set No 1003 is posed for official BR photographs. Headed by DMBS No S60005, with No S60004 on the rear, the other vehicles in the formation are TSLs Nos S60506, S60507 and S60508 and TF No S60702. Livery is unlined green with a light grey roof. The radiator covering (on one side only) is slatted, and large headcode numerals and blanks are prominent.
Colin J. Marsden collection

During the late 1940s and early 1950s, the number of passengers using Hastings line trains was increasing to the extent that the 'Schools' class steam locomotives were finding it difficult to cope with the heavy loads. Also, the existing coaching stock was not in particularly good condition, and new rolling stock based upon modified Mk1 stock was ordered for the route. The locomotive-hauled coaches were to be narrow-bodied for Hastings line gauge restrictions, and would have a shorter than standard 58ft underframe. Construction of 32 coaches was under way at Eastleigh works when a decision was taken to dieselise the line. Plans immediately changed, and the coaches were completed as trailers and powercars for seven six-car diesel-electric units, scheduled to commence working the more important business trains from the 1957 summer timetable. Considerable cost savings were made in this way, but really the 'new' trains were little more than a motorised version of existing steam-hauled stock. Choice of diesel-electric transmission for the trains was logical, as unlike other regions of BR, Southern Region staff were already trained in the intricacies of electric traction, and generators and traction motors powered in this way held no fears for them. In addition, the English Electric 4SRKT engine was already tried and tested on other types of motive power, and the same traction motor fitted in the Southern EMUs could be used. Once initial teething problems were overcome, the Class 6S units (later Class 201) settled down and gave very reliable service until their final days, when mixed formations started to appear in the same way as with the DMUs. Three units were disbanded in 1964, and the six powercars and some trailers were utilised until 1979-81 in six three-car hybrid units for the Reading-Redhill route, known as 'Tadpoles', after which the power cars were returned to the Hastings trains. The 'Tadpoles' are described under Class 206. After tunnel loading gauge clearances were improved, the Hastings route commenced electrified services from summer 1986, and the hard-worked Hastings DEMUs were displaced. Most went to breakers, Mayer Newman of Snailwell, but six Class 201 vehicles have been saved and are in various stages of preservation at St Leonards Railway Engineering. Two of the vehicles, Nos 60000 and 60501, are part of a five-car unit operated by Hastings Diesels Ltd. This is passed for main line running, and together with Class 202 vehicles Nos 60018 and 60529 and a Class 4CEP EMU trailer, works on both railtours and some services for the privatised train operating companies, currently on Anglia Railways, from Norwich to Great Yarmouth and Lowestoft.

The driver's cab of a Hastings DEMU was more or less the same as the contemporary Class 4EPB EMUs. The tip-up seat and foot rest cavity were not conducive to a very comfortable posture, but at least the facilities were an improvement on the footplate of a steam locomotive. The same layout, with just minor differences, is to be found on all the SR DEMU classes. *Ian Allan Library*

Following due ceremony, the first diesel service train to Hastings departs on time from Cannon Street station at 17.18 on 6 May 1957, formed of units No 1003 and 1004. In common with EMU stock built at Eastleigh, the units were fitted with air whistles above the driver's cab window, instead of the now standard two-tone roof-mounted warning horns.

First class accommodation in the Trailer First vehicles of the 'Hastings' sets was in compartments with side access doors, and the décor was quite luxurious. The moquette is red with grey patterning, with a matching carpet, and the reclining seats are designed not to impede the door opening when extended. All second class accommodation was in open saloons, until one first class compartment in each TFLK was downgraded to standard in spring 1980.
Colin J. Marsden collection

Second class open saloon seating in the Class 6S trailers was arranged two-plus-two facing, with table between, and initially at least was carpeted in red to match the upholstery. These were the fashions (and the expressions) of 1957! *Ian Allan Library*

In BR 'corporate blue' with half-yellow front-end warning panel, '6S' unit No 1001 passes Woolmer Green on 6 January 1968, forming a special train from Finsbury Park to Grantham to test riding qualities, particularly over the powered bogies of the driving cars. The bogies were eventually modified to alleviate some of the problem, but the quality of the ride always left something to be desired.
David Percival

After a period in BR 'corporate blue', the Hastings units generally were given blue and grey livery with full-yellow ends, which livened up their appearance to good effect. The original radiator cover slats tended to cause overheating and have been replaced with a mesh screen, and the original air whistle has been replaced by roof-mounted two-tone warning horns. Led by DMBS No S60011, Class 6S unit No 1006 hurries down Hildenborough bank on 12 May 1973, forming a standard service of the day between Charing Cross and Hastings. The 'S' of Class 6S signifies that these were 58ft short-wheelbase units, originally ordered for locomotive-hauled coaching stock. The later Class 6L and 6B units (Classes 202 and 203) were built with the standard BR Mk1 63ft 5in long-wheelbase underframe.

Six powercars and six trailers from units Nos 1002, 1003 and 1004 were used to provide vehicles for the Reading-Redhill Class 3R 'Tadpole' units in 1964. Spare trailer cars were integrated into set No 1007 to return it to a six-car unit, two trailers having been transferred to unit No 1032 after two of its original trailer vehicles were taken out and used for Departmental purposes. Following the serious Hither Green accident in November 1967, four Hastings unit trailers were considered as beyond economical repair and were scrapped in Hither Green depot yards during January 1969. This meant that two powercars could be used as spares for times when others were under maintenance. The two Class 201 vehicles, Nos S60004 and S60005, originally from set No 1003, were often formed into temporary sets with trailers from other units, and it was not unusual to see the short-wheelbase motor cars working with long-wheelbase trailers. Passing Frant on 10 August 1982, the spare powercars 'top and tail' the trailers from Class 202 (6L) unit No 1016, and form the 12.45 service from Charing Cross to Hastings.

The two spare Class 201 powercars could also be pressed into service as Departmental 'tractors', and on this occasion were operating with the High Speed Track Testing Coach No DB999550. Seen at Wimbledon, the vehicle was in use to test London Transport tracks between Fulham Bridge and Parsons Green, and also visited Richmond. *Colin J. Marsden*

Travelling between Grove Park and Hither Green on 9 October 1982, Class 201 unit No 1002 forms the 09.40 Hastings-Charing Cross train. As the floor-mounted engine takes up much space in the powercar, seating in these vehicles is restricted to 22. The three standard class trailers seat 52, and the trailer composite has provision for 36 in first class and six in 'standard'.

Displaying their Southern two-character route indicator codes '22' and '12', the 12.45 and 12.44 trains from Charing Cross to Hastings and Orpington, respectively, approach Waterloo East on 1 September 1983, formed of Class 201 Hastings unit No 1002 and Class 415/1 4EPB EMU No 5140.

Long and short-wheelbase 'Hastings' DEMUs pass at Mountfield sidings on 15 March 1986. Led by driving motor No S60005, unit No 1003 forms the 10.45 service from Charing Cross to Hastings, and No 1012 works the 11.33 from Hastings to Charing Cross. *John Scrace*

The two powercars from Class 201 'Hastings' DEMU No 1001 lead two six-car long wheelbase units, Nos 1011 and 1032, passing Brightside on 12 April 1986, forming the 'Long Thin Drag' railtour from London Victoria to Carlisle, via the Settle and Carlisle line. This view shows the varying roof conduits on individual vehicles, and also the stepboards below each individual door. *Les Nixon*

For a short time before EMUs took over the London-Hastings services, the DEMUs were branded with red marketing stickers, reading 'Ride the 1066 Route' and '1066 Country'. The logos were to help publicise the Kent and East Sussex area, and were the result of co-operation between the 1066 Development Panel and BR.

Their 30 years in service for BR having come to an end, a dozen 'Hastings' cars stand in Temple Mills yard on 6 September 1987, awaiting haulage to the Mayer Newman breakers yard at Snailwell. One powercar from Class 201 unit No 1007 leads the line.

Converted to Departmental 'Sandite' unit No 066, it was assured that the number '1' would be added for maximum 'Hastings' effect! Ex-Class 201 powercars Nos S60002 and S60003 are unusual exhibits at Colchester depot Open Day on 2 May 1988. Carrying Departmental numbers ADB977376/7, the vehicles are in use as 'tractors' for the London Transport Track Recording Coach No DB999666. Both DEMUs were broken up at Gwent Demolition, Margam, in March 1994.

At a ceremony performed inside St Leonards Railway Engineering depot on 28 September 1991, newly-restored Class 201 driving motor No S60000 was given the name *Hastings*. Standing alongside Class 50 No 50035 *Ark Royal*, the vehicle has been returned to original green livery and provided with a half-yellow front-end warning panel.

During a period when it worked the line in preservation, three-car 'Hastings' unit No 1001 *Hastings* rests at Tenterden Town, on the Kent & East Sussex Railway, on 5 March 1995. Two engine compartment window glasses await replacement.

Augmented with a Class 4CEP trailer, four 'Hastings' vehicles have been restored for main line running. On 15 March 1997, the Hastings Diesels Ltd unit passes Heath Junction, returning to Cardiff Central, after working a Cardiff Railway 'Valley Lines' service to Rhymney. The small blackened area on the roof betrays where the exhaust pipe protrudes through the centre of the engine room roof hatch. *Antony Guppy*

BR Eastleigh six-car Class 202

Built by:	British Rail Eastleigh Works	
Introduced:	May 1957	
Coupling Code:	None, but within SR DEMU types only	
Engines in each Driving Motor:	Two 500hp English Electric 4SRKT	
Transmission:	Electrical. Two nose-suspended axle-hung traction motors	
Body:	64ft 6in x 9ft 0in	
Weight:	DMBS	55 tons
	TSL	30 tons
	TFLK	31 tons
Operating numbers:	DMBS	60014 to 60031
	TSL	60521 to 60547
	TFLK	60707 to 60715
Renumbered:	60014 to 60152, 60015 to 60153	

The first seven Class 201 (6S) DEMUs were insufficient to allow for Hastings services to be completely dieselised, and a further nine six-car sets were constructed and delivered from Eastleigh works between May 1957 and March 1958. By this time, it had been realised that the standard BR Mk1 63ft 5in underframe could be used on the Hastings route, providing the coach bodies were kept to the same flat-sided design of the first batch. Thus, the units were classified 6L, the 'L' standing for long underframe. Outwardly, their appearance was the same as the earlier short-framed units, except they had four passenger windows in the driving motors instead of three, and eight windows in the trailer vehicles instead of seven. The Class 6L units started life in green livery, some had a short period in all-over blue, and they were then given the far more attractive blue and grey. Latterly, some vehicles reverted to original green, and the unit numbers were changed to comply with the practice of incorporating the class number with the operating number. In the same way as the Class 201 units, withdrawal from traffic resulted from electrification of the Hastings line, although some survived to be mixed and matched with Class 205 DEMUs. Three powercars are preserved, two currently restored and operational. Two TSLs are also passed for main line running, and other 'Hastings' vehicles are in various stages of restoration at the premises of St Leonards Railway Engineering.

Less than a year after entering service, Class 6L units Nos 1018 and 1016 head towards Somerhill tunnel from the Tonbridge stop, forming the 12.20 Charing Cross-Hastings train on 12 April 1958. *John N. Faulkner*

During 1958, experiments were carried out on some 'Hastings' units with a view to abolishing oil tail lamps. This was to be done by using special roller blinds in the rear headcode indicator. One of the experiments involved red and white diagonally-striped blinds, as shown here on Class 6L DEMU No 1015. The unit is rounding the curve at Bopeep Junction, between West St Leonards and St Leonards Warrior Square. *Ian Allan Library*

With DMBS No S60015 leading, Class 6L unit No 1011 forges up Hildenborough bank on 12 May 1973, heading for the Sevenoaks stop as a Hastings-Charing Cross train. Behind the three fixed forward windows, situated next to the driver's door on this side of the powercar, is a narrow corridor alongside the power unit, radiator grilles being on the opposite side.

A well-loaded 12-car evening peak service, the 17.40 from Cannon Street to Hastings, passes between Chislehurst and Petts Wood on 19 May 1975, formed of '6L' units Nos 1014 and 1016. The eight passenger windows in the trailer vehicles can clearly be seen, compared with seven on the shorter-framed Class 201s.

As the Class 202 vehicles were longer, the seating capacity also increased, the trailer second vehicles having provision for 60, the trailer firsts 48, and the motor brakes 30. Therefore, a complete six-car long-frame unit had a total of 288 seats, compared with 242 in the short-frame '201s'. On 4 August 1982, trailer standard No S60529 of unit No 1013 is seen at West St Leonards.

A reduction in first class travel on the Hastings route resulted in the side-corridor trailer first vehicles being modified to trailer composites. Two first class compartments were downgraded to provide 12 extra seats for standard ticket holders, seats in first class being proportionately reduced to 36. Trailer composite No S60709 is also a part of unit No 1013, at West St Leonards on the same day.

Carrying an unfamiliar headcode '96', the diverted 13.44 Hastings-Charing Cross train, passes New Cross Gate in pouring rain on 1 October 1983. The first-built long-frame Class 202 No 1011 leads No 1013. The two powercars in unit No 1011 were the last to survive in traffic, and to avoid a number clash with new Class 60 locomotives were renumbered from 60014 and 60015 to 60152 and 60153, respectively.

With only weeks to go before the services are electrified, Class 202 DEMU No 1012 leads the 14.33 Hastings-Cannon Street train, approaching Robertsbridge, on 21 March 1986. The regular '22' headcode changed to '33' for services to and from Cannon Street. Third rail for the electrified services is laid for EMUs to take over the Hastings diagrams from May.

Departing from the Etchingham stop on the same day, Hastings-bound Class 202 No 1018 forms the 12.45 train from Charing Cross. The six vehicles that made up this unit formation, remained constant during their lifetime, all being withdrawn at the same time in May 1986, and cut up at breakers Mayer Newman of Snailwell.

After the Hastings line electrification, Class 202 DMBS No S60022 from unit No 1015, had an extended lease of life replacing powercar No S60106 in three-car Class 205 unit No 1107. Heading trailer No S60656 and driving trailer No S60806, the slab-sided 'Hastings' vehicle, renumbered as unit 205007, approaches Clapham Junction on 2 May 1987, and with Class 207 DEMU No 207003, forms the 15.43 Uckfield/16.19 East Grinstead-Victoria train.

Class 202 unit No 1013 was the last complete six-car '6L' to remain in traffic. Renumbered 202001, it passes Coulsdon on 30 May 1987, at the rear of Class 207 unit No 207016. With powercar No S60019 facing the camera, the two sets form an empty coaching stock movement from New Cross Gate to St Leonards. *Alex Dasi-Sutton*

Preserved three-car Class 202 'Hastings' unit No 1012 visited the Swanage Railway on 30 June 1990, where leading driving motor No S60016 was named *Mountfield* by publisher Ian Allan. Restored to original green livery with a small yellow warning panel, the unit operated Purbeck Line trains to Harman's Cross in the ensuing summer months. *Andrew P. M. Wright*

Organised jointly by the Hastings Diesel Group and the Southern Electric Group, the 'Hastings Diesel Swansong' railtour of 8 August 1987 is formed by Class 202 set No 202001. Having visited Weymouth Quay, the train carefully threads its way back past cars and holidaymakers. *A. C. Smallbone*

A total of nine preserved 'Hastings' vehicles can be seen in this view inside the spacious St Leonards Railway Engineering depot on 28 September 1991. Nearest to the camera is TSL No S60528 from Class 202 unit No 1013.

DMBS No S60018 of Class 202 unit No 1013 was named *Tunbridge Wells* at a ceremony at Tunbridge Wells station on 12 May 1995. The vehicle was brought in from Hastings by a Class 73 electro-diesel, and later the train made a special run to Tonbridge. To meet current regulations, a front-end headlight has been fitted, and since being returned to the main line the number S60018 has been changed to S60118 to avoid duplication with a Class 60 locomotive.

Forming the 16.30 Cardiff Central-Portsmouth Harbour service train on 26 March 1997, the preserved 'Class 201' unit passes Bishton flyover, between Newport and Severn Tunnel Junction. Train operating company, South Wales & West Railway, as it then was, hired in the unit to supplement a number of extra trains needed in connection with a Wales vs England Rugby international at Cardiff Arms Park stadium. Class 202 DMBS No S60118 *Tunbridge Wells* leads.

BR Eastleigh six-car Class 203

Built by:	British Rail Eastleigh Works	
Introduced:	March 1958	
Coupling Code:	None, but within SR DEMU types only	
Engines in each Driving Motor:	Two 500hp English Electric 4SRKT	
Transmission:	Electrical. Two nose-suspended axle-hung traction motors	
Body:	64ft 6in x 9ft 0in	
Weight:	DMBS	55 tons
	TSL	30 tons
	TFLK	31 tons
	TRB	35 tons
Operating numbers:	DMBS	60032 to 60045
	TSL	60548 to 60561
	TFLK	60716 to 60722
	TRB	60750 to 60756

With the buffet car as the third vehicle and driving motor No S60039 leading, Class 6B unit No 1034 arrives at Tonbridge on 22 April 1961, forming a service from Cannon Street to Hastings. The original, and not unattractive, unlined green livery prevails. *Alec Swain*

To completely dieselise all the Hastings passenger diagrams, a final batch of seven six-car units was built, and delivered between March and May 1958. As a buffet car was included in place of one trailer second vehicle, they were classified 6B, and later became Class 203. Two TRB vehicles were removed from sets Nos 1031 and 1032 in 1964 and were converted for Departmental use. Other trailers were found from disbanded sets, and the units were reclassified 6L. Patronage of the buffet facilities generally was disappointing, and with the coming of modern health requirements, coupled with some structural problems, the remaining five vehicles were withdrawn from service in 1980. They were scrapped by Mayer Newman, Snailwell, in August 1982. The sets Nos 1033 to 1037, now without buffet cars, were reclassified 5L, but remained Class 203. Ex-Departmental buffet car No S60750 is the only Class 203 vehicle to have been preserved and awaits attention at St Leonards Railway Engineering.

The interior of a Class 6B buffet car in 1958, showing the serving counter, with the kitchen at the far end. Under a magnifying glass, the tariff board reveals that a cup of tea was six old pence (6d), a coffee 7d, a toasted teacake 4d, a beer 1s 3d, and a gin and tonic 2s 3d! *British Rail*

Labelled 'BUFFET', vehicle No S60756 of '6B' set No 1036 is also seen at Tonbridge during the early 1960s. Besides buffet and bar facilities, the TRB vehicles had provision for 21 seats, but unfortunately these were placed over the bogies, and often meant that drinking liquid refreshment could be something of a hazard! The 'pancakes' on the roof of the buffet car are air extract outlets from the kitchen. *Brian Haresnape*

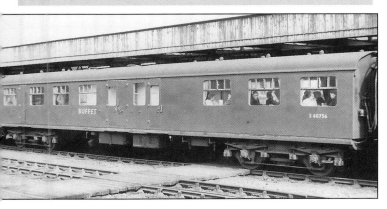

After the introduction of British Rail's new corporate image in 1965, units due for repainting were given all-over blue from mid-1966, with full-yellow cab ends added in 1967. However, before many 'Hastings' sets were so treated, 'Inter-City' blue and grey livery was extended to main line units and much improved their appearance. In short-lived BR 'corporate blue', Class 6B unit No 1036 passes near Crowhurst, forming a Charing Cross-Hastings train. It is in a form of matt blue which did not wear at all well, and has small coach number S60042 and a small BR logo. *Ian Allan Library*

'Hastings' DEMUs took over the Saturdays-only Brighton-Exeter through service from the summer timetable 1972. A Class 6B and a Class 6L were diagrammed to work the out and back trip together, travelling via Fareham, Southampton and Salisbury. Displaying headcode '11', DMBS No S60032 leads the return 13.50 Exeter-Brighton train arriving at Salisbury on 20 May 1972. Unit No 1031 now operates without its original buffet car, and has been redesignated '6L' Class 202. The rear unit is '6B' No 1036. *Geoff Gillham*

Two Class 203 units visited Great Eastern territory on 28 August 1971, Nos 1035 and 1037 seen here passing Reedham, returning to Eastbourne from Lowestoft. Facing the camera is DMBS No S60045 of unit No 1037, the last built in May 1958. The 1958-built units are distinguishable from the 1957 ones in that the trailers lack external lighting conduits on the coach roofs. *G. R. Mortimer*

Forming the 12.40 Charing Cross-Hastings service, Class 203 unit No 1035 bursts from Chislehurst tunnel on 16 May 1974, approaching Elmstead Woods. Driving motor No S60041 leads, and the third vehicle is the buffet car.

Class 203 (6B) powercar No S60045 leads unit No 1037 away from Cannon Street on 7 June 1976 and rounds the curve to Borough Market Junction. Bearing the correct headcode '33', the train is the 17.00 from the city terminus to Hastings.

On the same June day in 1976, the 17.16 train for Hastings awaits departure from Cannon Street, led by unit No 1032. This was the second Class 203 set to have its buffet car removed, and like No 1031 is redesignated as a Class 202 '6L' unit. The remaining five sets kept their TRB vehicles until 1980, but unlike sets Nos 1031 and 1032, they retained class number 203 after they were removed. This unit includes two short-framed trailer first vehicles, Nos 60701 and 60702, from disbanded Class 201 units.

Departing from Charing Cross on 14 September 1977, Class 203 unit No 1033 forms the six-car 12.15 train for Hastings. Since the 1980s, this view of the London terminus has changed out of all recognition, a massive development having been constructed in the air space above the station roof.

With buffet car No S60752 withdrawn, Class 203 unit No 1035 is now designated '5L'. On 4 August 1982, the five-car train approaches Battle as the 10.44 from Hastings to Charing Cross. From September 1985, it received trailer standard No S60559 from unit No 1036, and became a '6L' unit again.

A new depot for the 'Hastings' DEMUs was constructed at St Leonards, near West Marina station, and although convenient to Hastings, which was only two miles away, the building was very near to the sea. The sea air, coupled with sea water spray in rough weather, was a major factor in causing bodywork corrosion to the units in later years. Standing outside the five-road facility on 24 April 1985, DMBS No S60045 of Class 203 unit No 1037 awaits a new lease of life with Class 207 'East Sussex' DEMU No 1309, which it powered from 1985 until it was withdrawn with the unit in 1987-8. *British Rail*

From September 1985, Class 203 set No 1036 ran as a four-car formation (4L) for use between Tonbridge and Tunbridge Wells. Passing Tunbridge Wells Central Goods signalbox on 21 March 1986, the unit forms the 11.15 shuttle from Tunbridge Wells Central to Tonbridge.

Buffet trailer No S60755 was withdrawn from unit No 1031 in 1964, and after a period in storage was rebuilt in 1969/70 at Stewarts Lane depot as inspection saloon No TDB975025. Among the major modifications, the buffet and kitchen area were converted to a large saloon, and the end gangways were removed and observation windows fitted in the coach ends. It also received twin headlights and roof horns. In January 1991, the 'General Manager's Saloon', as it had become known, was repainted into the red, white, blue and grey colours of Network South East, and was usually hauled around the system by matching Class 73/1 electro-diesel No 73109 *Battle of Britain 50th Anniversary*. The combination is seen here at Stewarts Lane on 11 January 1991, in company with other '73/1s' No 73128 *O.V.S. Bulleid CBE* and No 73132.

The second buffet car withdrawn in 1964, No S60750 from unit No 1032, spent ten years out of service before being converted into a test coach for the Advanced Passenger Train (APT). It was used for experiments in tilting technology, for which it was particularly suitable due to its narrow body. Numbered RDB975386 'Laboratory 4' *Hastings*, it stands in Derby Technical Centre on 11 July 1990, mounted on APT-style tilt bogies.
Colin J. Marsden

Strictly, illustrations of unit No 203001 should be under the Class 202 heading, as all the vehicles in the set emanate from Class 202 No 1011. However, when the unit was reduced to four coaches, it was provided with a Class 203 unit preface, and appears in this section in an attempt to avoid confusion! Repainted into unlined green livery, but retaining a full-yellow end, the unit is seen in service on the Uckfield line on 26 September 1987. Driving motor No S60015 leads, and carries headcode '88', forming the 12.42 departure to London Victoria. *Les Nixon*

Another four-car unit comprising Class 202 vehicles from set No 1013 was identified by use of set number 203101. Unlike No 203001, which comprised two trailer standard vehicles between the two driving motor brakes, No 203101 was formed with one trailer standard and one trailer first. With DMBS No S60018 facing the camera, the '4L' unit stands at Crowborough station on 5 March 1988, working the 15.41 service from Uckfield to Oxted. *John B. Gosling*

BR Eastleigh three-car Class 204

Converted by:	British Rail Eastleigh Works	
Introduced:	July 1979	
Coupling Code:	None, but within SR DEMU types only	
Engines in each Driving Motor:	600hp English Electric 4SRKT	
Transmission:	Electrical. Two nose-suspended axle hung traction motors	
Body:	64ft 0in x 9ft 3in (Trailer 63ft 6in x 9ft 3ins)	
Weight:	DMBS	56 tons
	TS	30 tons
	DTCL	32 tons
Operating numbers:	DMBS	60102, 60103, 60107, 60121
	TS	77500, 77503, 77507, 77508
	DTCL	60802, 60803, 60807, 60821

After the Class 206 'Tadpole' units were disbanded in 1979, their former Class 2EPB EMU driving trailers were remarshalled between two-car Class 205 '2H' units to form a newly-designated Class 204 '3T' three-car DEMU for use on non-electrified lines in Berkshire, Hampshire and Wiltshire. The former EMU driving trailers were placed in the four units as the centre car, the redundant driving cab being rendered inoperative for safety reasons and locked. Also, the buffer heads were removed and the yellow ends repainted blue. Withdrawal of the units took place during 1987, and the last two in service by then, ran as originally constructed two-car sets, the trailers having been removed.

A few months after being formed at Eastleigh works, Class 204 '3T' DEMU No 1401 makes an empty coaching stock movement at Eastleigh on 11 April 1980. After reversing into the station, it will form the 16.27 stopping train from Eastleigh to Portsmouth & Southsea. Driving trailer composite No S60807 from Class 205 unit No 1121 is leading, the yellow line at cant-rail level showing the position of first class seating. This shows up well against the original all-over blue paintwork.

With ex-Class 205 DTC No S60821 from unit No 1122 facing the camera, Class 204 No 1402 approaches St Denys station on 7 July 1981, with the 16.15 local service from Southampton Central to Portsmouth Harbour. *Colin J. Marsden*

With DMBS No S60103 from Class 205 unit
No 1104 leading, Class 204 set No 1404
enters Bursledon station on 12 June 1982, as
the 12.23 train from Portsmouth Harbour to
Southampton. The black triangle on the front
of the motor brake vehicle signifies to station
staff the position of the brakevan.

Crossing the Broom Channel, just north of
Hilsea, Class 204 (3T) set No 1403 forms the
15.44 Salisbury-Portsmouth Harbour train on
12 June 1982. Blue and grey livery has
replaced the original all-over blue. DMBS
No S60102 from Class 205 unit No 1103
provides traction from the rear.

Arrival at Portsmouth Harbour station.
Class 204 DEMU No 1403 enters its allotted
platform on 14 May 1984, having departed
from Reading at 15.53. Alongside is Class 421
4CIG EMU stock, which has arrived as the
15.30 train from Waterloo.

With a small Network SouthEast branding on the bodyside, driving trailer No S60802 leads the 08.40 service from Salisbury to Portsmouth Harbour on 22 July 1986. The unit number now incorporates the class, and No 1403 has become 204003. *Chris Wilson*

Destined to be withdrawn from traffic in five months' time, '3T' unit No 204001 (ex-1401) passes Silchester on 21 March 1987, forming the 11.23 train from Basingstoke to Reading. After being removed from service in August 1987, the driving cars were scrapped at the premises of Mayer Newman, Snailwell. DTCL No S60807 succumbed in December 1988, followed by DMBS No S60107 a year later. *D. E. Canning*

Reformed as a four-car unit without the centre trailers, Class 204 units Nos 204004 and 204002 pass Wimbledon in heavy rain on 30 November 1987, working the 12.10 Waterloo-Salisbury duty. Only days later, a traction motor failure while working the same diagram resulted in these final Class 204 vehicles being withdrawn from traffic.

BR Eastleigh two- and three-car 'Hampshire' Class 205

Built by:	British Rail Eastleigh Works
Introduced:	August 1957
Coupling Code:	None, but within SR DEMU types only
Engines in each Driving Motor:	600hp English Electric 4SRKT
Transmission:	Electrical. Two nose-suspended axle-hung traction motors
Body:	64ft 0in x 9ft 3in (Trailer 63ft 6in)
Weight:	DMBS 56 tons
	TS 30 tons
	DTCL 32 tons
Operating numbers:	DMBS 60100 to 60125, 60145 to 60151
	TS 60650 to 60678
	DTCL 60800 to 60832
Renumbered:	60100 to 60154, 60101 to 60155

Prior to Beeching swinging his legendary axe, the Southern Region operated a sizeable network of non-electrified rural and branch line services. Most of them were worked by steam traction, and it was recommended in the BTC Modernisation Plan that diesel-electric railcars should replace them. A batch of 18 two-car units was constructed at Eastleigh works, and were placed into service in 1957 for use in the Hampshire area. They comprised a driving motor brake second saloon and a driving trailer composite, and were classified 2H for 'Hampshire' and numbered 1101 to 1118. Four more units were built in 1958 for the Ashford-Hastings line and the Bexhill West and New Romney branches, and these were numbered 1119 to 1122. Such was the success of the Hampshire dieselisation that four three-car units, Nos 1123 to 1126, were built in late 1959, and units Nos 1108 to 1118 were augmented to three coaches by the addition of a trailer second vehicle. The final batch of seven three-car units, Nos 1127 to 1133, were placed in traffic in 1962, for the Reading-Salisbury services. Although retaining a 3H classification, these were known as 'Berkshire' units and differed from the others in the class by having a larger guard's van,

which reduced the seating by 10. As branch lines in Hampshire were closed down, units became surplus and were transferred to other services, notably the Oxted line, from London to East Grinstead, and to Lewes and Polegate via Eridge. Two toilet compartments were provided in the driving trailer composite, as this vehicle contained the first class seats. Without gangway connections, passengers in the other coaches could not access the facility, at least while the train was moving. Unlike some DMUs of the period, modifications to alleviate the situation were never made, except in one rebuilt set No 1111, and eight vehicles that became part of the Class 204 units. Electrification of the Redhill-Tonbridge line, the Eastleigh-Portsmouth route, and the introduction of Class 159 and 165 units all contributed to the demise of the 'Thumpers' as they are affectionately known, and first withdrawals commenced in 1987. In addition to three vehicles used by Railtrack for track maintenance, 11 units (mainly three-car) are still in passenger operation with Connex South Central, and they could well see in the Millennium, while said Railtrack ponders the economics of electrifying its remaining routes to Uckfield, and between Ashford and Hastings.

Fresh from Eastleigh works, Class 2H 'Hampshire' DEMU No 1102 is posed for its official BR photograph on 19 August 1957. The engine is the same 500hp English Electric unit fitted in the 'Hastings' DEMUs. Livery is unlined SR green with light grey roof panels, and the engine compartment and guard's van can be seen to take up half the length of the motor brake. The white toilet window in the driving trailer composite is also apparent, situated next to the first class compartments. The vehicles are numbered S60101 and S60801, respectively. *Ian Allan Library*

The two first class compartments of a '2H' composite vehicle provided 13 seats, arranged three-a-side in one section and three-plus-four in the other. All had folding armrests on each side. Moquette is blue-grey/maroon, with the carpet monogrammed 'BR'. Later units had reclining seats fitted. *Ian Allan Library*

The second/standard class open saloon of the 'Hampshire' trailer units will be recognisable to anyone who travelled on Southern Region from the late 1950s onwards, the seating being the same as contained in the hundreds of contemporary electric multiple units of the times. They seated 104, with provision for another 50 in the driving trailer composite vehicles, and 52 in the motor brakes. *Ian Allan Library*

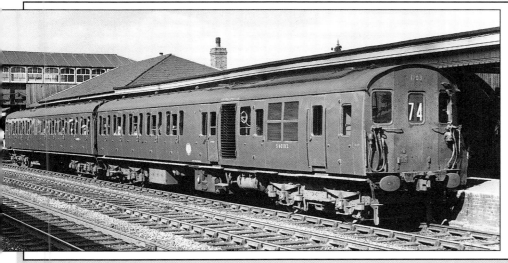

Comprising DMBS No S60102 and DTCL No S60802, Class 2H unit No 1103 stands at Eastleigh station, *circa* 1959, working an Andover to Southampton service. The roof panels have weathered down to a darker grey, and the whistle above the driver's window can be seen. The headcode panel allows for quite large numbers. *Ian Allan Library*

When reformed with a trailer and reclassified '3H', three-car 'Hampshire' sets had the original 500hp engine output increased to 600hp by using a larger Napier turbocharger. Led by motor brake No S60115, Class 3H unit No 1116 departs from Waterloo on 1 September 1962, working the 10.54 train to Salisbury, believed to have been the first appearance of a DEMU at the terminus. Prior to having an inverted black triangle on the unit end containing the guard's van, some driving motors were painted with a large fluorescent orange 'V', as shown here. *John Scrace*

Led by motor brake No S60110, Class 3H unit No 1111 is evidently fresh from Eastleigh works following overhaul, having had the roof panels restored to light grey. In addition, roof mounted two-tone horns are fitted to replace the original whistle, a small yellow front-end warning panel has been added with inverted black triangle, and the headcode panel shows much smaller numbers. On 20 June 1965, the three-car unit is seen at Basingstoke, working a Southampton-Reading train. In 1979, this unit was extensively refurbished and reclassified as '3H(M)'. *Alec Swain*

After withdrawal of services from the New Romney and Bexhill West branches, the two-car Class 2H units then remaining were transferred to the South Western Section of Southern Region. On a sunny 21 February 1967, set No 1124 leaves Micheldever station as a Reading-Southampton service. Third rail is in situ in preparation for electrified services between Waterloo and Bournemouth. *John A. M. Vaughan*

The first of the second batch of Class 2H DEMUs, No 1119, passes the level crossing at the north end of Appledore station on 5 September 1973, forming the 16.25 train from Ashford to Hastings. It has been repainted from original green to the new BR 'corporate' livery of blue with full-yellow end. Under the first TOPS computer classification, the four two-car sets Nos 1119-1122 were denoted '204', but Nos 1119 and 1120 became '205s' when the class number was reused for the '3T' sets formed in late 1979. Seemingly to confuse matters even more, the other two units of the second build, Nos 1121 and 1122, were re-formed as '3Ts' and retained the classification of '204'!

With driving trailer composite No S60812 leading, three-car Class 3H 'Hampshire' unit No 1113 restarts from the scheduled stop at Clapham Junction on 4 June 1975, forming the 15.09 train from Victoria to East Grinstead and Eridge. Originally a two-car Class 2H unit, trailer No S60662 was added to the formation in late 1959.

The first of the final batch of 'Southern' three-car DEMUs, Class 3H 'Berkshire' set No 1127 turns off the electrified Bournemouth main line at Worting Junction on 3 December 1977 and takes the West of England route under Battledown viaduct. Driving trailer No S60826 is leading and shows the smaller headcode panel fitted to the seven 'Berkshire' units, which have more up-to-date bodywork than the earlier Mk1 builds. The service is the 07.56 from Reading to Salisbury.

Before being reclassified as a three-car '3T' unit, what was then a two-car Class 204 DEMU, No 1122, approaches Southampton on 13 May 1978, forming the 10.42 train from Salisbury to Portsmouth & Southsea. With trailer added, the set became No 1402.

Passing beneath Southampton's once well-known signal gantry, Class 205 3H set No 1124 arrives as the 08.30 service from Portsmouth & Southsea. This was one of the four additional 'Hampshire' units added to the fleet in November/December 1959.

During 1979, Class 205 3H unit No 1111 underwent an extensive and experimental refurbishment at Eastleigh works and emerged as a Class 205/1 3H(M), standing for three-car 'Hampshire' modified. Gangway connections were fitted between the vehicles in the set, and fluorescent lighting, false ceilings and a public address facility were added. The first class section of the driving trailer was rebuilt as a standard saloon, the intermediate partition in the centre trailer was removed and the guard's van sub-divided. Seats throughout were to a revised profile and luggage racks were placed at cantrail level instead of being mounted above the seat backs. In addition, the driving desks were replaced in both cabs, and a four-position master controller included with an automatic engine starter. Also, the unit was able to operate in multiple with EMU stock. The high cost of the work, however, precluded other units being rebuilt in similar fashion. The first of the fleet to receive blue and grey livery, No 1111 departs from Rye on 17 August 1981, forming a Hastings-Ashford service. Entering the staggered station platforms is 'Tadpole' unit No 1206, described under Class 206.
John G. Glover

With driving trailer No S60824 leading, Class 205 'Hampshire' DEMU No 1125 approaches Portcreek Junction, near Hilsea, on 12 June 1982, forming the 15.04 train from Romsey to Portsmouth Harbour. The two driving vehicles have external cable conduits on their roofs, but the centre trailer which was constructed later, does not.

The final '3H' unit to be constructed in June 1962, set No 1133, leaves Portsmouth & Southsea station on 14 June 1982, forming the 15.58 service from Portsmouth Harbour to Reading. The front-end black triangle reveals that the motor brake, No S60151, is leading the unit, which is now in blue/grey livery. Of the three vehicles that made up a 'Berkshire' set, only the motor brake had roof conduiting.

All-blue motor brake No S60005 of Class 3R 'Tadpole' set No 1204 is pressed into service on the 13.40 Charing Cross-Hastings train on 22 August 1974, replacing the blue and grey powercar that would normally have been deployed on this otherwise all Class 203 formation, No 1035. Photographed passing Elmstead Woods on 22 August 1974.

On 17 July 1975, the same motor brake vehicle No S60005 is re-formed into standard '3R' unit No 1204 again, which looks particularly smart following a works visit. The 'Tadpole' approaches Redhill as empty stock to form the 17.09 train to Reading. Viewed from above, the differing width of the two types of vehicle is particularly noticeable.

'Tadpole' Class 206 set No 1205 enters the eastbound platform at Shalford on 19 May 1978, forming a Reading-Tonbridge train. With a plain yellow front end, motor brake No S60006 leads. Both this vehicle and the centre trailer emanated from Class 201 DEMU No 1004, while the driving trailer once formed half of Class 2EPB EMU No 5710. Unidirectional headcodes were used for this route, '55' used for Reading to Tonbridge, with '88' indicating a Tonbridge-Reading train. *Colin J. Marsden*

Propelled by motor brake No S60002, the 12.24 Reading to Tonbridge train trundles through the Surrey countryside near Nutfield on 22 April 1978. Ex-electric unit driving trailer No S77500 leads and clearly shows the odd mixture of one standard gauge high-density vehicle and two narrow-bodied 'Hastings' DEMUs.
Les Bertram

Once replacement of the Class 206 'Tadpole' units with Gloucester Class 119 DMUs got under way, the former 'Hastings' vehicles were overhauled and re-liveried in blue/grey in readiness for a return to the main line once again. The ex-EMU driving trailers were not required, however, and remained in all-blue, which explains the mismatch illustrated here. On 13 April 1979, unit No 1204 approaches Reigate as the 13.20 train from Guildford to Tonbridge.

Ex-Class 2EPB driving trailer No S77510 is all that now remains of the original Class 206 'Tadpole' unit No 1206, the two short-frame 'Hastings' cars having been re-formed into Class 201 unit No 1004. Spare long-framed motor brake No S60037 from Class 203 unit No 1033 and trailer No S60702 from unit No 1003 are now utilised for set No 1206, seen slowing for the Ham Street stop on 27 July 1982. The train is the 15.47 'Marsh Line' service from Hastings to Ashford.

One other unit categorised as a 'Tadpole' appeared for a short time from April 1986 to September 1987, three years after the original Class 206 sets were disbanded. Two surviving vehicles from Class 203 'Hastings' unit No 1037 and one from standard-bodied Class 205 'Hampshire' set No 1113 were temporarily coupled, and after running as unit No 1113 were given the number 206101. With motor brake No S60044 leading trailer standard No S60561 and driving trailer No S60812, the 13.05 train from Hastings to Ashford approaches Rye on 1 August 1987. Coupled to the rear to form six cars is gangwayed Class 205/1 3H set No 205101.
David Brown

BR Eastleigh three-car 'East Sussex' Class 207

Built by:	British Rail Eastleigh Works	
Introduced:	January 1962	
Coupling Code:	None, but within SR DEMU types only	
Engines in each Driving Motor:	600hp English Electric 4SRKT	
Transmission:	Electrical. Two nose-suspended axle-hung traction motors	
Body:	64ft 0in x 9ft 0in (Trailer 63ft 6in x 9ft 0in Weight)	
	DMBS	56 tons
	TCL	31 tons
	DTS	32 tons
Operating numbers:	DMBS	60126 to 60144
	TCL	60600 to 60618
	DTS	60900 to 60918

The fleet of 19 Class 3D 'East Sussex' DEMUs was constructed at Eastleigh as one batch between January and August 1962 for the Oxted and East Sussex lines, to operate mainly between London Victoria-East Grinstead/Tunbridge Wells and Brighton via Eridge (truncated at Uckfield in 1969). Three Bridges to Tunbridge Wells, and Tonbridge to Eastbourne via Heathfield were also a part of the original plan, but passenger services on both routes were soon withdrawn. The units were technically similar to the Class 3H 'Berkshires', but due to restricted clearances in the tunnels at Tunbridge Wells, were designed with a body width 3in less than the other units. They also incorporated some modifications: the driver's cab desk was to a revised design, and the cab ends were of steel-reinforced fibreglass with rounded corners, with recesses for the connecting jumper cables and hoses. The diesel engines were not readily interchangeable with the same types in other units, as although being of the same model, they were mounted differently. Also, the first class seating and the lavatory compartment were in the centre trailer instead of the driving trailer. The body styling showed some influence from the BTC Design Panel, but tradition prevailed regarding an absence of gangway connections between vehicles, and again only

passengers in the centre trailer had access to the toilet when the train was on the move. Significant withdrawals resulted after the East Grinstead electrification, half the fleet being taken out of traffic in the late 1980s and mostly broken up at Mayer Newman of Snailwell and Vic Berry of Leicester. Four units were transferred to Eastleigh depot in 1989 to replace withdrawn 'Hampshires', until the 'Solent Link' electric service joining Portsmouth with Southampton and Eastleigh was completed. Further inroads were made in the early 1990s, and the trailers were withdrawn from three sets which were then reclassified 207/1. Like the Class 205/1 described under the appropriate section, all three '207/1s' were then provided with a redundant Class 411 4CEP EMU trailer and became Class 207/2. Together with just one remaining two-car Class 207/0, all the sets now operate 'Marsh Line' trains between Ashford and Hastings/Eastbourne, and two units have been named. After abortive attempts to electrify the Ashford-Hastings route, it was announced by Railtrack in March 1998 that work in this respect should be completed by the year 2002. On this basis, like the Class 205s, the 'East Sussex' DEMUs could well remain in traffic well into the Millennium.

The first Class 3D DEMU built for the Oxted line, No 1301, climbs away from Alton on 14 March 1962, on a test run from Eastleigh works and back. The 'Oxted' sets, as they became popularly known in their early years, were three inches narrower in width than the standard-bodied 'Hampshire/Berkshire' units, but having a curved body profile, they did not impart a slab-sided effect like the earlier 'Hastings' trains. With recessed housings for the jumper cables and hoses, a handrail around the front end below the windows, and more modern-looking styling, the units are easily recognisable. The light grey roof on this first unit was not maintained on the remainder of the build, and stepboards were fitted before it entered traffic. *C. Small*

With motor brake No S60143 leading, Class 3D DEMU No 1318 leads another unit of the same class on 18 May 1963, approaching Woldingham. The six cars form the 12.09 service from London Victoria to Tunbridge Wells West, and provide total seating for 368 passengers. The centre trailer accommodated 42 in second class and 24 in first, the driving trailer 76 in second only, and the motor brake 42. The headcode '22' given to Southern Region Central Division Victoria-Tunbridge Wells West trains was the same as allocated to SR Eastern Division for Charing Cross-Hastings diagrams. Stepboards are fitted, and at first these ran the length of each coach. *John Scrace*

On 22 March 1964, '3D' unit No 1315 makes the prescribed stop at Rowfant, forming the 13.08 train from Three Bridges to East Grinstead. The initial all-over green livery did not look very inspiring, particularly when not kept clean. Two-tone green on the BRCW Type 3 locomotive (later Class 33) alongside looks far more attractive. Rowfant station closed in January 1967 and services on the branch ceased. *G. D. King*

With a half-yellow front-end warning panel added to the original green paintwork, driving trailer No S60909 leads 'Oxted' unit No 1310 on a misty 1 January 1967, at Hartfield. The train is leaving for Forest Row and East Grinstead (High Level), one of the last workings before the line between Ashurst Junction and Three Bridges closed to passengers on the following day. *John A. M. Vaughan*

Two women on each side of the level crossing attempt a conversation above the rasp of engines, as Class 207 DEMU No 1311 departs from Uckfield on 6 May 1980, with driving trailer No S60910 at the rear of the 13.12 service to London Victoria. British Rail 'corporate blue' was not really an aesthetic improvement on the original green livery of these sets, but at least the front ends were enlivened by the yellow paint prescribed for easier sighting by track workers. Unfortunately, this also highlighted the recessed jumper cable housings, as these quickly became blackened with an accumulation of grime and dead insects. The painted yellow band at cant-rail level on the centre trailer shows the position of the first class seating. Individual stepboards for each compartment are now in place.

Having completed the Clapham Junction stop, two three-car 'Oxted' units start away again on 9 May 1981 and head the 12.13 train from London Victoria to East Grinstead and Uckfield, the sets dividing at Hurst Green. Motor brake No S60137 leads unit No 1312 and shows the non-radiator side of the engine compartment with fixed windows instead of grilles. The front-end cable recesses have been recently cleaned, probably when the inverted black triangle, to show which end the luggage compartment is placed, was added. The '3D' unit classification is stencilled on the left of the recess, with 'SE', indicating the depot allocation, on the other side.

Slowing for the Winchelsea stop, DMBS No S60133 leads Class 207 DEMU No 1308, and forms the 17.27 train from Hastings to Ashford on 27 July 1982. The much more attractive blue and grey livery has now been applied. The old station building is now a private residence.

A pastoral scene at Birchden Junction, near Eridge, on 19 April 1984 as Class 207 DEMU No 1312 passes as the 09.14 train from London Bridge to Uckfield. Driving trailer No S60911 is leading. The line to the right went to Groombridge and Tunbridge Wells West stations, both closed by BR in July 1985, and now part of the Spa Valley Railway. *Paul Shannon*

On 24 April 1985, unit No 1305 growls along the single line between Grove tunnel and Tunbridge Wells West, motor brake No S60130 leading the 14.09 service from Tonbridge to Eridge. The short pipe protruding from the roof above the engine compartment, is the exhaust outlet. The twin roof-mounted horns are also clearly shown.

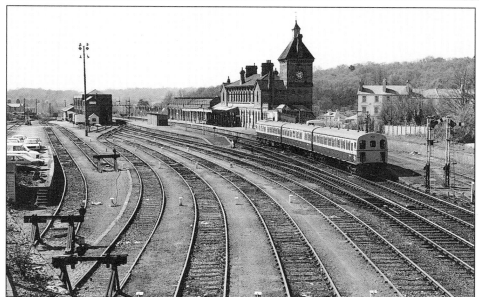

On the same day a few months before services were withdrawn, Class 207 unit No 1305 pulls away from Tunbridge Wells West station, forming the 14.57 service from Eridge to Tonbridge. The fine old 1866 station buildings are now a restaurant, and the remainder of the once extensive station complex is occupied as a Sainsbury's supermarket.

Renumbered with the unit identity as a prefix, Class 207 set No 207011 (ex-1311) approaches the staggered platforms at Rye on 26 July 1988, forming the 15.15 train from Hastings to Ashford. Only the powercars of the units had external roof conduiting, the two trailer cars being uncluttered in this respect.

Class 207 unit No 207002 (ex-1302) stands inside Selhurst depot on 30 August 1988, painted into Network SouthEast sector livery of red, white, blue and grey. With the 'S' prefix now omitted, motor brake No 60127 faces the camera and displays two front-end unit numbers at waist level in place of the single set number above the headcode panel applied previously.

On 18 July 1990, Eastleigh-based Class 207 set No 207005 hurries along the single line near Gillingham (Dorset), working the 18.30 train from Yeovil Junction to Basingstoke. Only seven of the original total of 19 'East Sussex' units survive at this date, three allocated to Selhurst depot and four to Eastleigh. A small NSE logo is apparent below the headcode panel of driving trailer No S60904. Centre trailer No S60604 was later removed from the formation and withdrawn in July 1991. As a two-car unit it was transferred back to Selhurst depot, reclassified '207/1' and renumbered 207102. In 1995, a centre trailer was restored to the formation from an EMU, and the unit in this guise still currently operates, renumbered for the third time as Class 207/2 No 207202.

Flanked by two Class 415 4EPB electric units, the first of the '207' fleet of DEMUs, No 207001 departs from the NSE South Central Sector terminus platforms of London Bridge on 18 August 1989. Still in blue and grey livery, the set has formed the 08.42 train from Uckfield, and now departs for Selhurst depot as empty stock for cleaning and servicing.

The 15.58 train from Hastings to Ashford accelerates away from the Rye stop on 6 June 1992, formed of Class 207/1 unit No 207101 and Class 205/1 'Hampshire' No 205025. The 'Oxted' unit has lost its centre trailer, received a new headlight and has been renumbered from 207004. Motor brake No 60129 leads.

A number of diesel unit types operated the Kensington Olympia-Clapham Junction shuttle services during the early 1990s, while problems with electrifying the route were resolved. Even 'East Sussex' units put in an appearance, No 207013 working what was intended to be the last diesel-powered 'Kenny Belle' on 23 July 1993. At the Olympia platform, motor brake No 60138 heads the last train of the day, the 19.00 to Clapham Junction. As well as a headlight being fitted, it has also been unofficially named *Ajax*.

With Ashford-Hastings 'Marsh Line' services planned to be extended to Eastbourne and Brighton, three two-car Class 207/1 'Oxted' units and one two-car 'Hampshire' set (described under the Class 205 section) were each provided with a centre trailer from Class 411 4CEP EMUs that had been reduced in formation from four cars to three; the new classification for '207/1s' was Class 207/2. With the centre vehicle now of wider proportions than the driving cars, motor brake No 60130 leads the newly-formed set No 207202 on 24 May 1995, passing between Ashford and Ham Street and forming the 11.22 service from Ashford to Hastings. The work to modify these units was undertaken at the Eastleigh works of Wessex Railcare (now Alstom). Gangway connections from the DEMU vehicles to the ex-EMU trailer were made, reducing seating capacity a little, and a repaint was ordered. The latter is evident as the jumper cable recesses are still yellow!

Reclassification of three 'East Sussex' units to Class 207/1, and then to '207/2', left one two-car set remaining, No 207017 becoming Class 207/0. On 24 May 1995, it leads Class 205/1 No 205101 as the 12.22 train from Ashford to Hastings and passes Bromley Green, near Ham Street. Without toilet facilities or gangway connections, it was not intended to use either of these sets for the extended diagrams to Eastbourne and Brighton.

To launch the extended Ashford-Hastings 'Marsh Line' timetable to Eastbourne and, initially, Brighton, two of the three Class 207/2 sets dedicated to the services were named at Ashford on 3 June 1995. With guests in period costume, No 207201 was unveiled as *Ashford Fayre*, and No 207202 as *Brighton Royal Pavilion.* The large cast nameplates are carried on the motor brake vehicles Nos 60129 and 60130, respectively.

Departing from the now newly-named Ashford International station, the only unnamed Class 207/2 DEMU, No 207203, forms the 11.22 train to Hastings on 28 November 1995.

Displaying headcode '21', driving trailer No 60901 leads unit No 207203 past an old loading gauge near Ham Street on a wintry 27 January 1996. The train is an extended 'Marsh Line' service, the 14.48 from Ashford to Brighton.

Metropolitan-Cammell six- and eight-car 'Blue Pullman' Class 251

Built by:	Metropolitan-Cammell Carriage & Wagon Company
Introduced:	November 1959
Engines in each Driving Motor:	One North British/MAN L12V18/21BS 1,000hp per car
Auxiliary engine in Motor Trailer:	One Rolls-Royce eight-cylinder C8N 190hp per car
Transmission:	Electrical, two GEC frame-suspended traction motors driving through Brown-Boveri spring drive
Body:	Driving Motor Brakes 66ft 5½in x 9ft 3in
	Motor Trailers/Non-motor trailers 65ft 6in x 9ft 3ins
Weight:	DMBF/DMBS 67 tons 10cwt
	Non-driving MPSL and MKFL 45 tons 10cwt
	TKFL and TPFL 33 tons
Operating numbers:	DMBFL 60090 to 60093
	DMBS 60094 to 60099
	MPSL 60644 to 60649
	MKFL 60730 to 60733
	TKFL 60734 to 60739
	TPFL 60740 to 60749

The 'Blue Pullmans', as they quickly became known from their 'Nanking' blue livery, were totally different from anything that had operated on BR before. A part of the 1955 Modernisation plan, the two six-car and three eight-car 90mph trains were built at the Washwood Heath works of Metro-Cammell and were an attempt to combat the new postwar luxury introduced on UK domestic airlines. In addition, there was a need to provide alternative services to Birmingham and Manchester, while the main line from Euston was disorganised by the electrification work of the early 1960s. Three separate trains were devised, the 'Midland Pullman' from St Pancras to Manchester Central, the 'Birmingham Pullman' from Paddington to Birmingham Snow Hill and Wolverhampton Low Level, and the 'Bristol Pullman' between Paddington and Bristol Temple Meads, via Bath. The trains were the first for public service provided with full air-conditioning, and in addition passengers enjoyed a high standard of sound and thermal insulation with fully enclosed gangway connections, double-glazed windows, wall-to-wall carpeting, and comfortably-styled modern seats and tables. To keep weight down on the driving motor brake vehicles, only the rear bogies were motored, the adjacent bogies on the coupled trailers at each end of the trains also having motors fitted to power the air-conditioning, lighting and kitchens. The six-car sets were for first class passengers only, and were formed of a driving motor brake at each end, a motorised kitchen car divided in half with seating, two luxury open firsts called parlour cars, and another kitchen car. The eight-car units provided both first and second class seats. The two powercars were motor brake seconds and were each attached to a motorised parlour car second. A trailer kitchen first came next, and this in turn was attached to

two parlour firsts and another trailer kitchen. The original classifications for the BR TOPS computer were:

251/1	Driving Motor Brake First with lavatory
251/2	Driving Motor Brake Second
261/1	Non-driving Motor Parlour Second with lavatory
	Non-driving Motor Kitchen First with lavatory
261/2	Trailer Kitchen first with lavatory
	Trailer Parlour First with lavatory

A major problem with the 'Blue Pullmans' was the Swiss-designed Schlieren bogies that were fitted. These gave an excellent ride under various coach types on the other side of the English Channel, but appeared to dislike BR track intensely, causing hard and constant vibration, with a tendency to the occasional violent lurch — not appreciated in the dining cars! Various attempts at modification were unsuccessful, and when electrification between Euston, Birmingham and Manchester was completed in 1966, the London Midland Region soon transferred its two sets to the Western Region. They were modified at Swindon works in 1967, with multiple-unit jumper cables added to the driving car front ends, and with some first class seating downgraded to second. In this guise, they formed a 12-car train on the busy morning and evening 'Bristol Pullman'. The eight-car 'Birmingham Pullman' sets were switched over to operate a 'South Wales Pullman'. As non-standard trains, their days were numbered, and although repainted into a new grey and blue livery, they were all withdrawn in May 1973. None have been preserved.

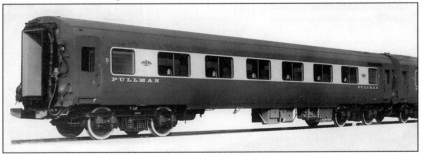

With both the background and the foreground of the print retouched
to white, trailer parlour first No M60741 is posed for an official Metropolitan-Cammell photograph at Washwood Heath, soon after manufacture in November 1959. The complicated-looking array of jumper cables between the cars within each unit are apparent around the Metro-SIG gangway connection. *Ian Allan Library*

Led by driving motor brake No M60090, the first six-car 'Midland Pullman' set stands at Cricklewood during trials early in 1960. Delivered in November 1959, staff had to be trained in all aspects of the new Pullman operation, and the first service train did not run until July 1960. All first class, the six-car units seated 132 passengers. *Colin J. Marsden collection*

Appearing to be traversing a single track branch line, the second 'Midland Pullman' unit, with driving motor brake No M60092 leading, is in fact on trials near Hendon late in 1959. The train is running over the stretch of line at Silkstream Junction, where the fast and slow lines are separated. Livery is 'Nanking' blue with white for the window areas, with the nose-ends displaying a new version of the Pullman Company crest in gold and red. *Colin J. Marsden collection*

Forming the 08.50 'Midland Pullman' from Manchester Central to St Pancras, one of the two LMR six-car 'Blue Pullman' units passes near Bedford in August 1961. Three warning air horns are fitted below the buffer area, one on the left and two on the right. The buffer shanks are painted red and the two outer headlights have disc brackets below them, presumably for white discs to be fitted in case of a lighting failure. Behind the round casing between the buffers is a drawhook for emergency coupling. *Colin J. Marsden collection*

The interior of a first class trailer parlour saloon. The white button below the armrest enables the seat back to recline, and beside the table lamp is a call button to summon an attendant. On the wall next to the window, a handle controls the operation of the venetian blind, the blades of which are between the two double-glazed panes of glass. Upholstery and carpeting are red. *Ian Allan Library*

At Old Oak Common on 10 September 1960, DMBS No W60097 shows off the two 'Pullman' brand names on the Western Region sets, and the Pullman badge within the white paintwork around the windows. The front half of the vehicle is taken up by a full-width driving cab, a 32ft compartment for the power, control and cooling equipment, and a guard's compartment that includes an office and a stowage area. What remains is 18 second class seats arranged on a two-plus-one basis. These were the only vehicles of the six different types constructed not to have toilet facilities. *R. C. Riley*

The 'Blue Pullman' driving cab layout. The four large dials are, respectively, the brake cylinder pressure gauge, main reservoir/brake pipe pressure gauge, speedometer and main generator ammeter. The two handles on either side of the desk are the brake controller and the main power controller. Other controls relate to the window wiper, cab heating, engine start/stop, horn, and front-end lighting. *Ian Allan Library*

With whitened buffer heads, the 12.10 'Birmingham Pullman' from Paddington to Birmingham, passes near West Ruislip at speed in the early 1960s. With one stop at Leamington Spa, scheduled arrival time at Snow Hill station for the Western Region eight-car train is 14.05. *C. R. Lewis Coles*

In many ways, a precursor for the InterCity 125 units that would later pass this way, an eight-car 'Blue Pullman' set sweeps through Slough on 10 October 1963. The train is the 10.05 'Bristol Pullman' from Paddington, scheduled to arrive at Temple Meads station at noon. *R. C. Riley*

Led by driving motor brake second No W60098, the 14.30 'Birmingham Pullman' awaits departure time at Birmingham Snow Hill station on 28 March 1961. *Michael Mensing*

Although it was to be another six years before 'South Wales Pullman' services began, a Western Region eight-car 'Blue Pullman' visited Swansea on 6 September 1961, with a press trip from Paddington. It made a stop at Port Talbot, where it stands at the temporary platform built there while extensive alterations took place, both to station and trackwork.
John N. Faulkner

Led by DMBS No W60097, the 14.30 'Birmingham Pullman' arrives on time at Paddington on 14 September 1962. Total seating in the eight-car Pullman trains was 108 first class and 120 second class.
C. R. Lewis Coles

The evening 'Bristol Pullman' departure from Paddington was timed at 16.55, and omitting the stop at Bath, was due to arrive at Temple Meads in ten minutes under two hours, at 18.45. During the journey, the kitchens could be expected to produce 114 meals in the case of the Western Region, and 66 in the LMR sets. An eight-car train awaits departure time at Paddington in May 1963.
Brian Haresnape

The 18.10 'Midland Pullman' for Manchester Central awaits custom at St Pancras on 14 May 1964. Each of the all-first class seats could be reserved, a Pullman conductor meeting each passenger on arrival, and advising on seat location within the train. A precursor of the 'Eurostar' and 'Gatwick Express' services today.

Looking particularly modern compared with the '5600' class GWR 0-6-2T it is passing, the Paddington-bound 07.00 'Birmingham Pullman' from Wolverhampton Low Level, passes West Ruislip at speed on 21 September 1963. *C. R. Lewis Coles*

When the two Midland Region six-car sets were transferred to the Western Region in 1967, they were modified at Swindon works to operate in multiple as a 12-car unit. Multiple-unit jumper cables were added to the driving car front-ends, and some first class seating was downgraded to second. They operated together on the busy morning and evening 'Bristol Pullman' services, but worked individually during less busy periods. One of the six-car trains passes West Ealing on 5 June 1967, heading for Paddington. Now with an all-yellow front warning panel, it has lost its attractive Pullman crest.
John N. Faulkner

Operating together as a 12-car train for the peak evening 'Bristol Pullman', the two six-car units approach Paddington on 16 June 1970, as an empty stock working from Old Oak Common. Besides full yellow fronts, the BR corporate identity programme standardised blue and grey for main line passenger rolling stock. The BR 'monastral blue' was entirely different to the attractive 'Nanking' variety of the 'Blue Pullmans', and is now in reverse position, with the blue around the window areas and the remainder of the bodywork grey. Other modifications for multiple working are apparent in this view, which shows how the bodywork between the buffers has been cut away for a screw coupling to be fitted. Also, the three air-horns are now grouped together beneath the left buffer, and have had protective baffle-plates fitted.
John N. Faulkner

Passing Llansamlet on 17 June 1971, the eight-car 16.20 'South Wales Pullman' service from Swansea to Paddington, is led by driving motor brake No W60096. *A. Wyn Hobson*

The eight-car 'Blue Pullmans' were not altered for multiple-unit working, as few station platforms could accommodate a 16-car train, and few services would have warranted one. When the mandatory full-yellow front-end warning panels were introduced, the 'Blue Pullmans' without their nose-end crests, never really looked the same again. Unusually used for a special charter, an eight-car unit is at Carmarthen on 25 April 1970, operating from Surbiton to Newcastle Emlyn! The headboard obscuring one marker light, reads 'Gilks-Grenside Educational Special No 8'. *John N. Faulkner*

Nearly a year after being withdrawn from traffic in May 1973, an eight-car ex-'Blue Pullman' set languishes outside Swindon works on 9 April 1974. The vehicles were bought for scrapping by breakers T.W. Ward of Briton Ferry and G. Cohen of Morriston, and all were reduced to scrap by the summer of 1975. *Barry J. Nicolle*